OCS Study
MMS 2001-025

Coastal Marine Institute

Wind and Eddy-Related Circulation on the Louisiana/Texas Shelf and Slope Determined from Satellite and In-Situ Measurements

October 1993-August 1994

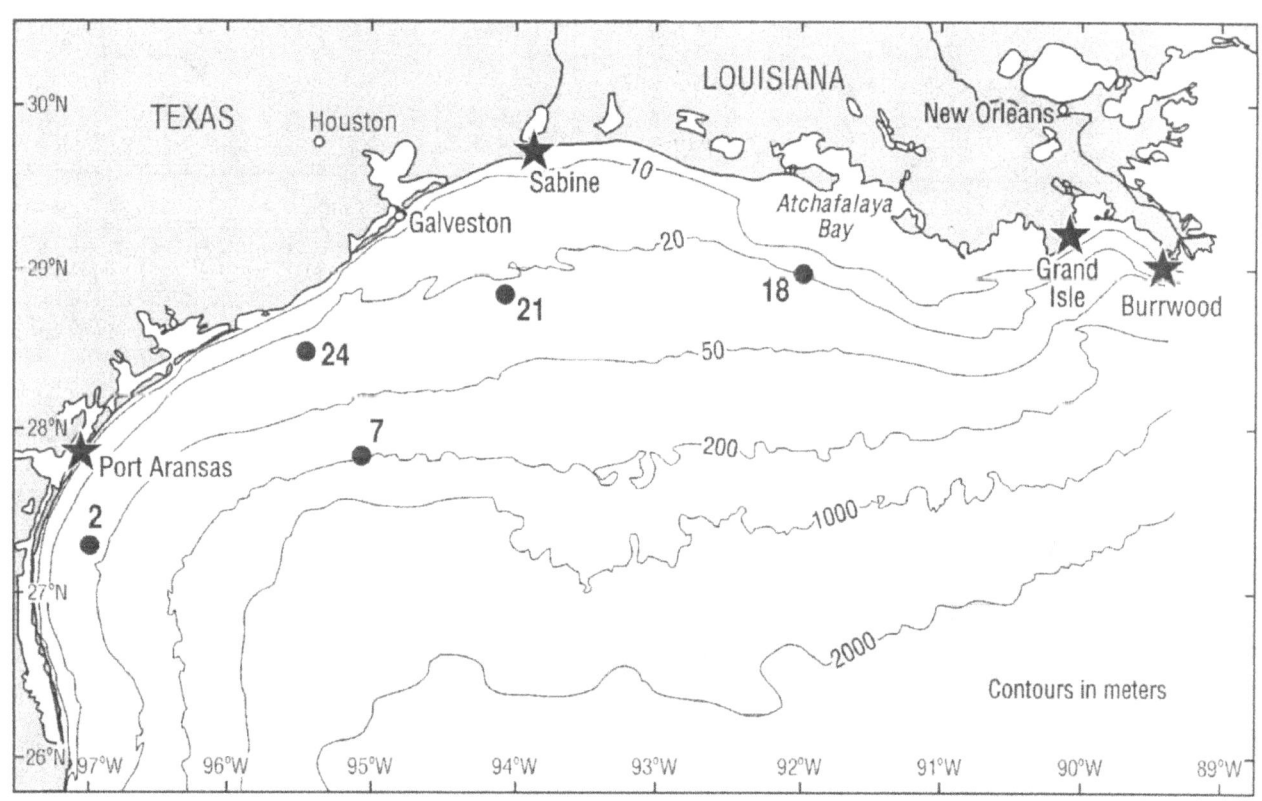

U.S. Department of the Interior
Minerals Management Service
Gulf of Mexico OCS Region

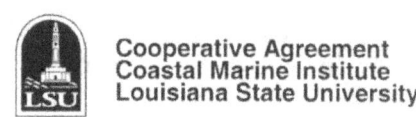
Cooperative Agreement
Coastal Marine Institute
Louisiana State University

OCS Study
MMS 2001-025

Coastal Marine Institute

Wind and Eddy-Related Circulation on the Louisiana/Texas Shelf and Slope Determined from Satellite and In-Situ Measurements

October 1993-August 1994

Author

Nan D. Walker

March 2001

Prepared under MMS Contract
14-35-0001-30660-19942
by
Coastal Studies Institute
Howe-Russell Geoscience Complex
Louisiana State University
Baton Rouge, Louisiana 70801

Published by

U.S. Department of the Interior
Minerals Management Service
Gulf of Mexico OCS Region

Cooperative Agreement
Coastal Marine Institute
Louisiana State University

DISCLAIMER

This report was prepared under contract between the Minerals Management Service (MMS) and Coastal Studies Institute, Louisiana State University. This report has been technically reviewed by the MMS and approved for publication. Approval does not signify that the contents necessarily reflect the views or policies of the Service, nor does mention of trade names or commercial products constitute endorsement or recommendation for use. It is, however, exempt from review and compliance with MMS editorial standards.

REPORT AVAILABILITY

Extra copies of this report may be obtained from the Public Information Office (MS 5034) at the following address:

U.S. Department of the Interior
Minerals Management Service
Gulf of Mexico OCS Region
Public Information Office (MS#5034)
1201 Elmwood Park Boulevard
New Orleans, Louisiana 70123-2394

Telephone Number: (504) 736-2519 or
1-800-200-GULF

CITATION

Suggested citation:

Walker, N.D. 2001. Wind and eddy related circulation on the Louisiana/Texas shelf and slope determined from satellite and in-situ measurements: October 1993-August 1994, OCS Study MMS 2001-025. U.S. Dept. of the Interior, Minerals Mgmt. Service, Gulf of Mexico OCS Region, New Orleans, La. 58 pp.

TABLE OF CONTENTS

LIST OF FIGURES

LIST OF TABLES

I. INTRODUCTION

The Louisiana-Texas Shelf Physical Oceanography Program (LATEX), sponsored by the Minerals Management Service, was funded to improve the understanding of circulation and associated causal mechanisms on the Louisiana and Texas continental shelves. Circulation in this region is complex as it is influenced by several time-varying environmental factors including wind forcing, river discharges, and the location and intensity of detached Loop Current warm-core eddies. During the LATEX field measurement program many valuable datasets were collected which individually revealed some aspects of circulation on the continental shelf and slope of Texas and Louisiana from April 1992 to December 1994. In this project, an attempt was made to further the understanding of near-surface shelf and slope circulation processes in the northwest Gulf of Mexico (GOM) by synthesizing several datasets collected during the LATEX field measurement period. The datasets included in this analysis included NOAA AVHRR sea-surface temperature (SST) imagery, TOPEX and ERS-1 sea-surface height (SSH) data, SCULP surface drifter data and LATEX-A current meter and temperature measurements. The NOAA satellite SST image data provided regional synoptic views of SST distributions over the LATEX shelf and slope when skies were relatively cloud-free. Shelf and slope circulation features such as the effluent plumes of major rivers, offshelf flow features (squirts), and Loop Current rings were identifiable and trackable in relatively clear-sky imagery. The SSH information, in the form of 10-day synthesis maps, depicted the locations and intensities of warm-core rings and cold-core eddies in the study region, information which is weather-independent. The SCULP surface drifters provided knowledge on lagrangian surface circulation patterns. The satellite datasets provided crucial information on the location and movements of shelf and slope oceanic features with which the drifter trajectories could be more accurately interpreted. The LATEX-A current meter measurements provided time-series measurements simultaneously at key locations on the LATEX shelf, enabling a more thorough investigation of the impacts of wind forcing on inner shelf circulation.

The Loop Current and the large warm-core eddies which separate from it dominate the circulation on the continental slope and deeper GOM regions (Elliot, 1982; Forristall et al., 1992). In this study warm core eddies and warm core rings will be used interchangeably. These warm core eddies typically have diameters of 200-400 km and maximum surface currents of 100-200 cm/s (Huh and Schaudt, 1990; Cooper et al., 1990; Forristall et al., 1992). Eddies usually separate from the Loop Current after it has surged north beyond 27° N latitude (Forristall et al., 1992). The frequency of eddy shedding varies between six and fifteen months (Maul and Vukovich, 1993; Sturges, 1994). During the LATEX field measurement program (2.75 year duration), six warm-core Loop Current eddies (Eddy T to Eddy Y) were observed in the northwestern Gulf of Mexico. After an eddy is shed from the Loop Current, it usually moves slowly westward at about 4 km/day until it reaches the western Gulf of Mexico shelf where it is constrained by shoaling topography in the western Gulf of Mexico in what has been commonly termed an "eddy graveyard" (Biggs, 1992). Thus, warm-core eddies often dominate circulation patterns in the western Gulf of Mexico (Cochrane, 1972; Elliot, 1982; Lewis and Kirwan, 1985). Vidal et al (1992) documented the collision of a warm-core Loop eddy with the Mexican slope near 22° N, when approximately 1/3 of the eddy's volume was lost. Eddy-related circulation in the western and northwestern Gulf of Mexico is thought to drive much of the surface current variability on the outer continental shelf (Oey, 1995). These warm-core eddies have longevities of several months to a year and, therefore, several Loop Current eddies may be found in the western Gulf of Mexico simultaneously (Biggs, 1992). Although less well studied, cold-core eddies (50-150 km in diameter) are often found in association with the warm-core eddies (Merrell and Morrison, 1981; Brooks and Legeckis, 1982; Hamilton, 1992). They do not often have a surface thermal signature and, thus, are not easily observable in NOAA satellite imagery. Our knowledge of the prevalence and movements of cold-core eddies in the Gulf of Mexico has mushroomed with recent improvements in satellite altimetry processing techniques in the Gulf of Mexico (Leben et al., 1993; Biggs et al., 1996).

Although circulation over the Louisiana/Texas shelf (Location, Figure 1) is complex and can vary rapidly, certain general circulation patterns have been determined from previous studies. On the inner shelf (< 30m water depth) west of the Atchafalaya Bay, surface circulation is primarily wind-driven and strong coherence has been found between alongshore wind-stress and alongshore currents for coastal locations (Smith, 1978; Crout et al., 1984; Lewis and Reid, 1985; and Cochrane and Kelly, 1986; Murray, 1998). This relationship results primarily in downcoast (westward) flow for much of the year with a coastal-type jet on the inner shelf (Cochrane and Kelly, 1986; Murray, 1998; Nowlin et al., 1998). A distinct surface flow reversal occurs during mid-summer when strong southerly winds prevail along the south Texas coast and weak southerly and southwesterly winds blow along the Louisiana coast (Cochrane and Kelly, 1986, Jarosz et al., 1996; Murray, 1998). The Atchafalaya and Mississippi River effluent plumes are discharged onto the inner shelf along the Louisiana coast (Figure 1). These buoyant outflows exhibit annual cycles with strongest flow onto the shelf in spring and weakest flow in late summer and autumn. The river effluents produce relatively cool, low-salinity, turbid water masses which are identifiable along the coast for much of the year using the visible and thermal infrared channels of the NOAA satellites (Rouse and Coleman, 1976; Walker and Rouse, 1993; Walker et al., 1994; Walker et al., 1996; Walker, 1996).

Cochrane and Kelly (1986) suggest that a cyclonic gyre is a dominant feature of the prevailing shelf circulation. The inshore limb of the gyre is the wind-driven coastal jet. Several authors have suggested that a convergence of coastal currents occurs where the wind-driven downcoast and wind-driven upcoast flows meet (Watson and Behrens, 1970; Smith, 1980; Cochrane and Kelly, 1986; Barron and Vastano, 1994). This convergence zone has been hypothesized to move north and south seasonally in concert with wind forcing changes. Cochrane and Kelly (1986) suggest that an eastward-flowing current occurs along the shelf edge as the seaward flank of the shelf-wide cyclonic gyre. Oey (1995) uses a numerical model to show that the convergence zone on the western flank of the gyre and the eastward shelf-break current are driven by collision and stalling of westward propagating Loop Current eddies in the northwest Gulf of Mexico, rather than wind forcing. The data synthesis proposed should provide an improved picture of the time and space variability of this convergence zone as well as the forcing mechanisms for it.

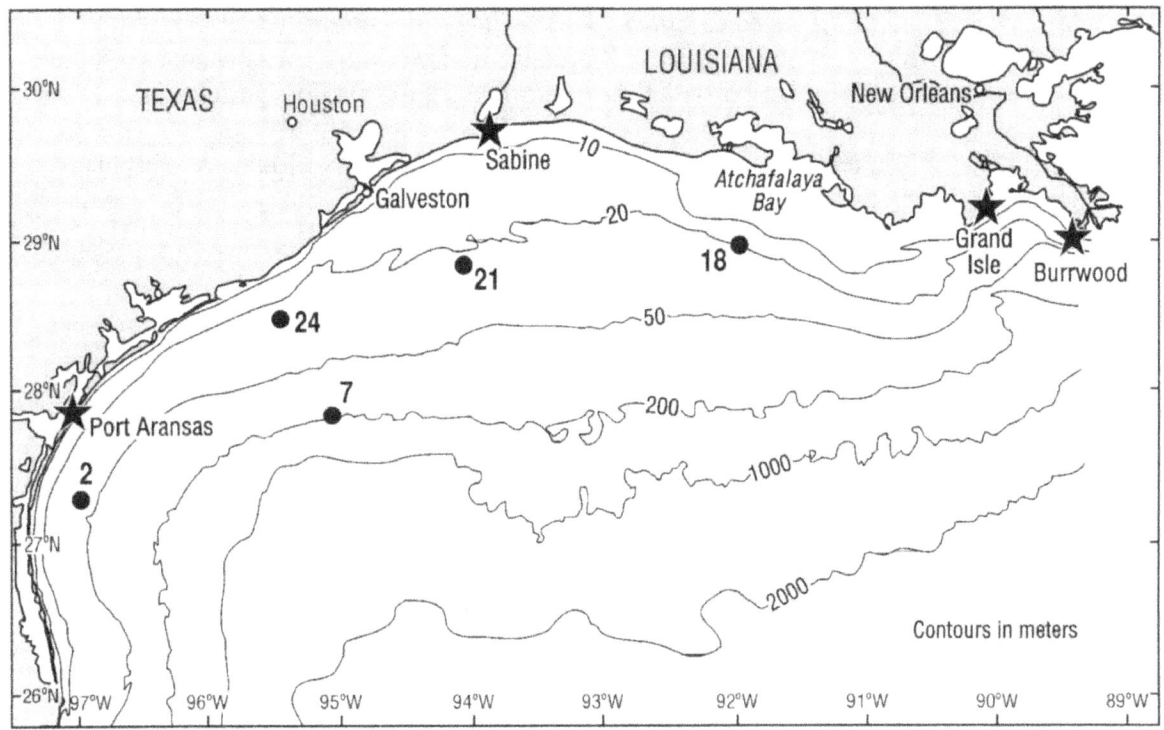

Figure1. Location map of the Louisiana/Texas (LATEX) continental shelf and slope depicting the locations of the meteorological measurements and the LATEX current meter moorings used in this study.

The goal of this research was to use selected high quality measurements obtained during the LATEX project from October 1993 through September 1994 to obtain a better understanding of synoptic-scale and seasonal-scale variations in surface and near-surface circulation on the Louisiana/Texas continental shelf and slope and the primary forcing mechanisms for the identified patterns. Key questions to be answered in this study included:

1. How do temperature fronts associated with the coastal current effect near-surface circulation? Do the drifters cross the density front associated with the coastal current or align themselves parallel to it? Does the front provide a barrier to onshore flow and do the drifter tracks change as the thermal front weakens in spring?

2. What does the synthesis of datasets reveal about the Texas convergence? How permanent is the convergence and what does the data synthesis reveal about its forcing mechanisms?

3. How do anticyclonic (A) and cyclonic (C) circulation features and A/C eddy pairs affect circulation on the shelf and slope in the LATEX region? Are there preferred areas for off-shelf flow? What are the surface velocities associated with the off-shelf flow features?

4. What new information is revealed about the coherency of summer upcoast flow along the LATEX shelf? How long does it last? Is it predictable from wind stress changes? Is there a convergence zone and resultant off-shelf flow during the up-coast flow period?

5. What is the spatial extent of upwelling along the Texas and northern Mexican shelf? How are the regional flow patterns affected by the eddy field?

II. METHODS

A. Satellite Image Data

Satellite sea-surface temperature (SST) measurements, obtained by the NOAA AVHRR (Advanced Very High Resolution Radiometer), were used to detect shelf and ocean circulation features of interest in this study. The 1.1 x 1.1 km spatial resolution (at nadir) and the multi-daily coverage provide a powerful source of information when cloud-cover was sufficiently low. These data were received via antennae from the NOAA satellites 4 to 8 times/day by equipment at the Earth Scan Laboratory, Coastal Studies Institute, LSU.

All satellite imagery received at the Earth Scan Laboratory were archived automatically after capture on 4 mm tapes during the LATEX project. All image processing and analyses were performed using the Terascan™ software provided by SeaSpace, San Diego, California which runs on an SGI Challenge computer server linked to X-terminals and Linux workstations. Sea surface temperatures were computed using a modification of the MCSST technique described in McClain et al (1985). A sobel filter enabled the detection and mapping of SST fronts. The workload for this project was reduced considerably by using archived imagery during the LATEX project. Most of the imagery used in this research project were individual images. However, in a few instances, compositing was performed with images space within 72 hours of one another. The compositing was performed using the warmest pixel technique and the imagery was renamed to reflect the use of two image datasets.

B. Satellite Altimetry Data

The sea surface height anomaly data from the LATEX field measurement period were produced by Dr. Bob Leben at the Colorado Center for Astrodynamics Research Dept. of Aerospace Engineering Sciences (CCAR), University of Colorado, Boulder and were made available to LATEX researchers via an anonymous ftp site (Bob Leben, personal communication). TOPEX and ERS-1 satellite data were used to create 10-day anomaly maps which were referenced to the OSUMMS95, a mean sea surface calculated at the Ohio State University by Dick Rapp and Yuchan Yi (Leben, personal communication). This mean sea surface was based on TOPEX, ERS-1 and Geosat data. Standard corrections were applied to the data and the "orbit" error was removed from both the TOPEX and ERS-1 data using a tilt and bias adjustment. The TOPEX and coincident ERS-1 data were mapped every 10 days using a spatial/temporal Cressman weighting scheme (Leben, personal communication). For selected events, the contoured height anomalies were superimposed on clear-sky satellite imagery to enable comparison of the synoptic SST features with the 10-day estimates of the sea surface height fields. The SSH data was particularly useful in mapping the warm rings and cold-core eddies within the NW GOM. The SSH data were available during two time periods during the study period: November 17-Decemver 12, 1993 and May 5, 1994-August 27, 1994. Unfortunately, the analyses were not available during the intervening period.

C. Drifter Data

From October 1993 through October 1994, approximately 300 ARGOS drifting buoys were released on the Louisiana shelf during the MMS-sponsored SCULP drifter program (Johnson and Niiler, 1994). Daily positions of these surface drogued (1 meter depth) drifters (at 1115 UTC) were available to LATEX researchers as ASCII files. The drifter data were reformatted and superimposed on the satellite SST data to aid in the interpretation of circulation processes and to further our understanding of the influence of prominent oceanographic features on surface circulation.

D. LATEX-A Current Meter and Temperature Data

The LATEX-A current meter and temperature measurements were extracted from the CD-ROM NODC-92 produced by Texas A&M under contract to the Minerals Management Service. The data had been quality controlled before release. The moorings chosen for study were based primarily on the circulation patterns revealed by the SCULP drifter data. The coastal current circulation regime was investigated using the top meters at mooring 2 (37 m water depth, 11m instrument depth), mooring 21 (25 m water depth, 14 m instrument depth), mooring 24 (26 m water depth, 8m instrument depth) and 18 (22 m water depth, 12m instrument depth). Thus, the inner shelf current meters were not all representative of near-surface flow as they were located 8-14 m from the still-water surface in 22-37 m water. Mooring 7 (200 m water depth, 14 m instrument depth) was near the shelf break in the region of the Matagorda squirt. Mooring 1 temperature data was used to investigate coastal temperatures associated with the summer upwelling regime. The locations of these moorings are shown on Figure 1. A 40-hour Butterworth filter was used to remove tidal effects from the current meter measurements.

E. Meteorological Data

Wind measurements from three C-MAN stations were used to characterize the wind field over the study area. Stations included Burrwood, LA, Sabine, LA and Port Aransas, TX. Hourly data were obtained from the National Data Buoy Center. Comparison of wind data from Burrwood and Grand Isle revealed that the Burrwood data better reflects wind stress over the coastal ocean as it is not as affected by land effects (sea-breezes, land-breezes). The Burrwood wind speeds were reduced to 10-m using the power law and an average neutral condition value of 0.12 for P (Hsu, 1988). The winds were resolved into vector components with an oceanographic orientation. Throughout the text, wind directions are referred to according to the direction they are blowing. East-west components are positive to the east. North-south components are positive to the north. A 40-hour Butterworth filter was used to remove tidal effects from the wind data. In addition, 10-years of climatological temperature data were analyzed for Grand Isle, LA and Port Aransas, TX.

III. RESULTS AND DISCUSSION

A. Winter Season Circulation Processes

1. Summer to Winter Shelf Cooling and Evolution of Surface Thermal Fronts

Continental shelf waters in the northern Gulf of Mexico cool substantially during autumn and winter as a result of increases in latent (evaporative) and sensible heat losses to the atmosphere and reductions in the incoming solar radiation (Nowlin and Parker, 1974; Huh et al., 1978). The cooling is more extreme and rapid in coastal waters where the heat storage capacity is less due the relatively shallow depths. A ten-year climatology of coastal surface temperatures for Grand Isle, LA and Port Aransas, TX (Locations, Figure 1) demonstrate the autumn cooling and spring warming that produces a distinct annual temperature cycle along the Louisiana/Texas coastline (Figure 2). Monthly-averaged temperatures range from maxima of 30° C in August to minima of 14° C in January. The monthly-averaged temperatures at the Louisiana and Texas sites were surprisingly similar. A comparison of water and air temperatures at each site revealed that the annual cycle of coastal water temperatures followed the annual cycle of the air temperatures closely; however, the monthly-averaged water temperatures were 1-2° C above the air temperatures throughout the year.

The regional chilling of coastal and continental shelf waters from summer to winter 1993/94 was investigated using satellite-derived measurements of surface temperature. The clear-sky imagery used to study the cool-down phase were obtained after cold-front passages on September 29, 1993, November 28, 1993 and January 4, 1994. Sea-surface temperature distributions on November 28, 1993 and the locations of the six profile lines from which SST measurements were extracted are shown in Figure 3. The temperature measurements for the six profile lines are shown in Figure 4.

On September 29, 1993 surface temperatures across the entire Louisiana-Texas shelf ranged from 29-31° C except near Atchafalaya Bay where minimum temperatures were near 25° C (Figure 4). The relatively low temperatures were probably related to the discharge of river water onto the shelf. However, other mechanisms have been identified that can also explain the cooler shelf waters in this region. The shallower bays chill more rapidly than the shelf and the wind behavior during cold-front passage events force bay water onto the shelf causing additional chilling of shelf waters seaward of Atchafalaya Bay.

By November 28, 1993, two months later, substantial changes in temperature had occurred across the continental shelf and particularly in coastal regions. The coastal and inner shelf regions had experienced cooling of 12 to15° C whereas the outer portions of the shelf cooled 5 to 8° C. Lowest surface temperatures (circa 12° C) were observed seaward of Atchafalaya Bay and in shallow nearshore environments due to the local discharge of relatively cool river water. Along the middle and southern reaches of the Texas shelf, minimum coastal temperatures were 15° C. Downstream from the Atchafalaya Bay system, there was a continuous band of cold inner shelf water ranging in temperature from 12° to 16° C. The coastal temperatures at the time of this image were about 1.5° C colder than the climatological means for November (Figure 2).

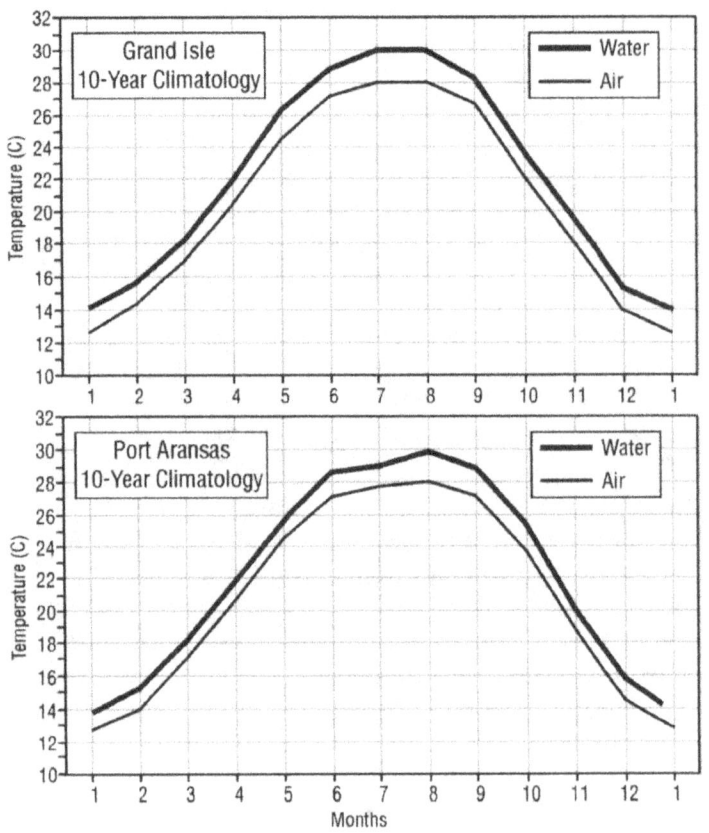

Figure 2. Climatological coastal air and water temperatures for Grand Isle, LA and Port Aransas, TX (1985-1994).

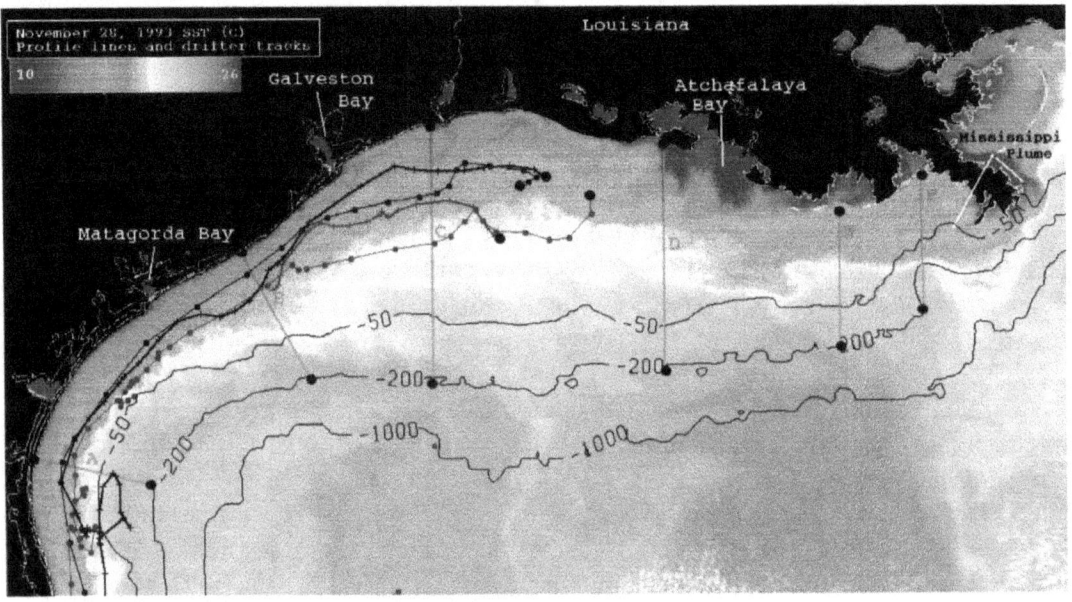

Figure 3. NOAA AVHRR satellite image of SST acquired on November 28, 1993. The locations of profile lines A-F are shown and daily positions (solid dots) of four SCULP drifters in the coastal current.

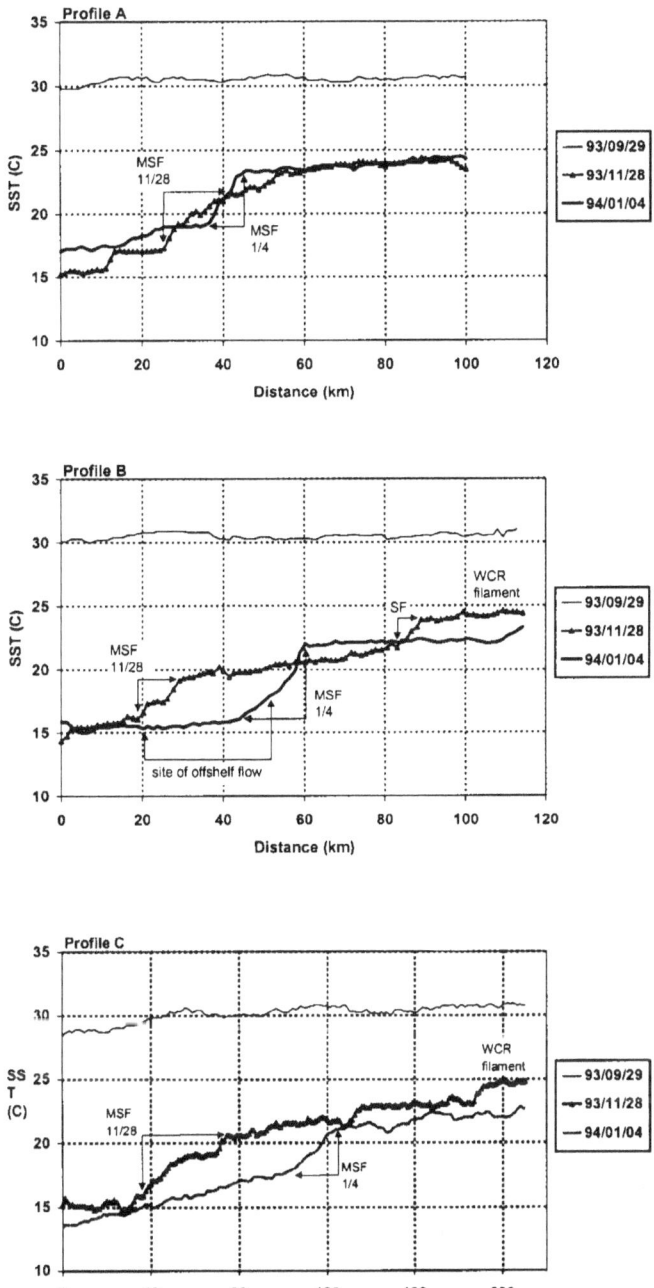

Figure 4. SST data extracted from 6 profile lines (Locations, Figure 3) on September 29, 1993, November 28, 1993 and January 4, 1994. January 8 data was substituted for line E due to excessive cloud cover on January 4. The distance is measured from the coastline. MSF denotes the main shelf front, SF denotes a shelf front and WCR denotes a warm core ring.

9

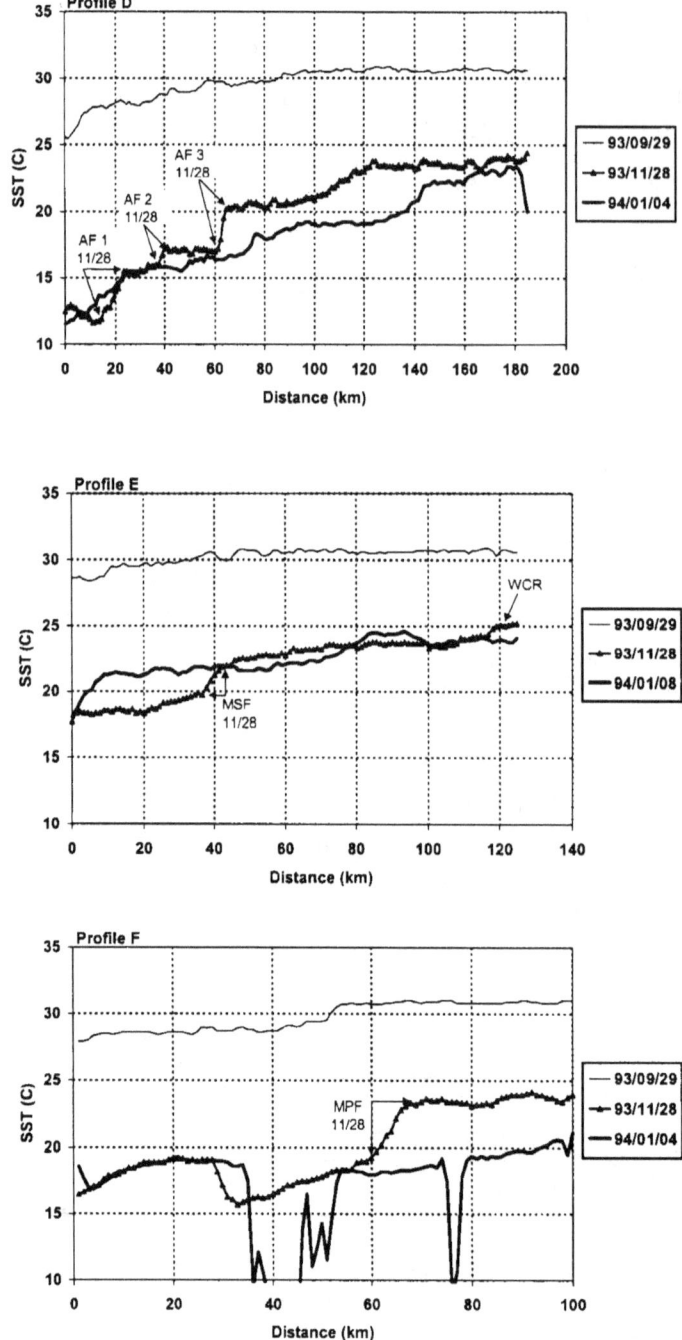

Figure 4. (continued). SST data extracted from 6 profile lines (Locations, Figure 3) on September 29, 1993, November 28, 1993 and January 4, 1994. January 8 data was substituted for line E due to excessive cloud cover on January 4. The distance is measured from the coastline. AF denotes Atchafalaya front, MSF denotes main shelf front, WCR denotes a warm core ring and MPF denotes the Mississippi plume front.

10

The temperature profiles extracted from the November 1993 image revealed the existence of cross-shelf temperature fronts particularly in the inner shelf regions (See Lines A, B, C, D of Figures 3, 4). The satellite imagery demonstrated that these fronts were associated with the Mississippi and Atchafalaya River effluents and the coastal current west of the Atchafalaya Bay system and along the Texas coastline. In some locations, surface fronts were associated with the warm waters of warm core eddies and filaments (See lines B, C, D, E, F of Figures 3, 4). The intensity of inner and mid-shelf fronts exceeded 3° C/10 km (0.3° C/km) along lines A, B, D, E and F. The sea surface temperature gradients were distinctive (4-6° C in 10 km, 0.4°C-0.6°C/km) across the Mississippi River plume front, south of the Southwest Pass effluent (Line F) where river waters abutted against warmer slope waters over the Mississippi Canyon (Figures 3, 4). Along this line, a weaker front was observed between the relatively cool river waters and the inner shelf waters. Seaward of Atchafalaya Bay, along line D, multiple fronts were detected. These sharp surface frontal features along line D may reflect a sequence of northerly wind-driven pulses of Atchafalaya River and bay water onto the inner shelf. The sharpest of these fronts were located 16 km and 63 km from the bay mouth (Figure 4). The front at 63 km measured 3.25° C/3 km (1.1° C/km). Along the northern Texas coast (Lines A, B, C), surface temperature fronts intensified as the shelf narrowed moving southward (Figure 4). Near Sabine (Line C), where the inner shelf is relatively wide, surface thermal fronts were relatively weak. The main shelf front along line C spanned the region between 38 and 78 km from the coast with a mid-point at 58 km. Along line B, the main shelf front was located 20-30 km from the coast. Along line A, the main shelf front was located between 25 and 40 km from the coast. The warmest portion of the inner shelf was along Line E, between the discharge plumes of the Mississippi and Atchafalaya Rivers, where inner shelf waters were 18° C and waters along the shelf break were near 25°C due in part to the proximity of a recently formed warm core ring (Figure 4). Temperatures near the shelf break were 24-25° C where filaments of warm core ring waters were encountered due to the presence of two in the NW GOM.

Between November 28 and January 4, 1994, the rate of cooling on the inner shelf was much reduced. Cooling of 1-3° C occurred in selected locations across the region. Along Line A, the main shelf front had intensified and moved seaward several km. Inner shelf temperatures along line A were slightly warmer in early January (Line 4). Along line B, cooling of 3-5° C was experienced 25-50 km from the coast. This temperature change corresponded with a region of significant off-shelf flow termed the Matagorda squirt and is discussed in detail in the next section. The main SST front moved seaward by about 30 km from November 28 to January 4. Cooling of about 1-2° C was experienced on the outer reaches of Line B. Along Line C, (Figure 4) cooling was greatest in the middle shelf region, between 40 and 120 km from the coast. This cooling may reflect advection of cooler waters into the region in addition to transfer of heat to the atmosphere. Seaward of Atchafalaya Bay (Figure 4), inner shelf temperatures were similar at the times of the November and January images, however, cooling of 2-4° C was detected 60-140 km from the coast. Along Line E, little surface temperature change was observed, except for warming of 2-3°C inshore. Near the Mississippi delta region, cooling of 3-5° C was experienced on the outer shelf. The inner shelf temperatures were relatively unchanged. The middle shelf region was cloud-covered (temperatures below 10° C), hindering additional comparisons along this line.

11

2. Surface Circulation Processes: Drifting Buoy Analyses

The tracks of drifting buoys released on the Louisiana/Texas shelf between October 15, 1993 and January 31, 1994 were studied in relation to the location of SST fronts and the position of oceanographic features as revealed by the satellite SST and SSH data. The drifters were released at various positions on the continental shelf seaward and west of the Atchafalaya River outflow. A few were released on the shelf west of Sabine (92°W). Water depths for the releases varied between 15 and 50 m. The drifters initially moved towards the west (Figures 3, 5). Several drifters that were released in mid-October during a period of southeast winds exhibited a trajectory that was distinctly northwestward, in the direction of the wind stress. Upon encountering the sharp SST front extending along the Texas inner shelf about 25-30 km from the coast, the drifters turned towards the southwest, subsequently moving parallel to this SST front. The drifters moved downcoast along the seaward side of the surface front, indicating the existence of a spatially extensive convergence zone along the surface temperature front.

The drifters that were released from October 1993 through January 1994 exhibited a wide range of circulation patterns (Figure 6; Table 1). However, two major and two minor shelf circulation patterns were identified on the Louisiana/Texas shelf within the 1st month of release (Figure 6a-d). The two major flow pathways identified during the October-January period are shown in Figure 5 and Figure 6a,b. The first major circulation pattern was down-coast flow within the coastal current along the Louisiana/Texas inner shelf passing the Texas/Mexican border at 26° N (Figure 6a). Another large group of drifters initially moved within the coastal current, but then turned eastward southeast of Matagorda Bay (Location, Figure 1), between 95 and 96° W where they flowed off-shelf along the 28° N parallel of latitude, between the 50 and 100 m isobaths (Figure 6b). Some of these drifters (and others) exhibited a sluggish cyclonic circulation pattern on the mid-shelf region centered around the 50m isobath (Figure 6c). The forth group moved directly south off the shelf onto the slope and into deeper Gulf region (Figure 6d). This group generally was deployed further offshore.

Wind behavior from October 1, 1993 through January 31, 1994 at three stations along the Louisiana and Texas coasts, Burrwood, LA; Sabine, LA and Port Aransas, TX, (Locations, Figure 1) are shown in Figure 7. These graphs of wind displacement show net southwestward wind stress, explaining the predominance of westward and southward currents (down-coast) along the Louisiana/Texas inner shelf. The winds appear much stronger at Burrwood. There were 20 days of missing data at Port Aransas, prohibiting a quantitative comparison of wind speeds from this graph. The occurrence of winter storms or cold-front passages are revealed as reversals in the wind or as short-lived rotational features in the wind record diagrams. The duration of southward winds during winter storms varied from one to several days. The wind history during this 4-month period is typical of autumn and winter, when the frequency of southwestward winds along the Louisiana coastline increases and predominates (Rhodes et al., 1985; Walker and Hammack, 2000).

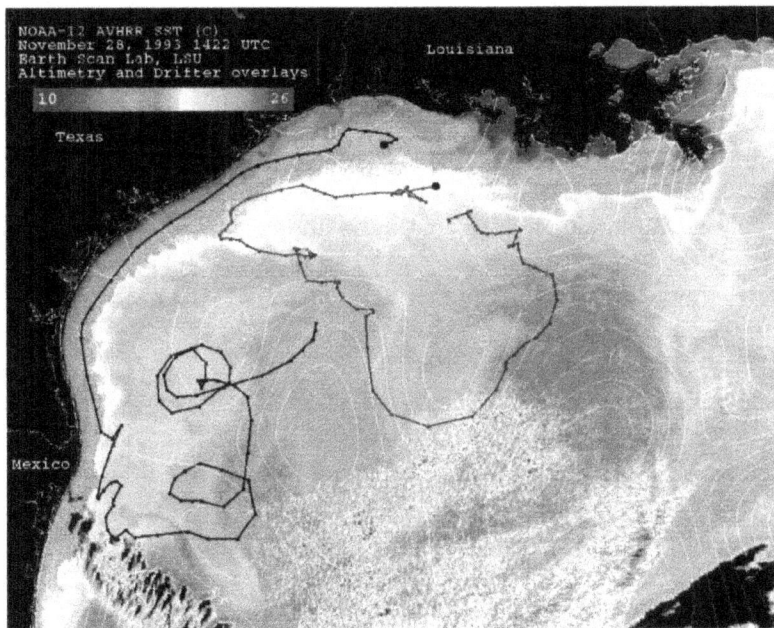

Figure 5. Satellite image of SST (C) with SSH anomaly contours (cm) superimposed. Positive anomalies are highs (anticylonic eddies) and negative anomalies are lows (cyclonic eddies). Tracks of two SCULP drifters are shown, depicting different paths taken by drifters in the 11/ 1993-1/1994 period. Daily positions are indicated with small dots and deployment sites with larger dots.

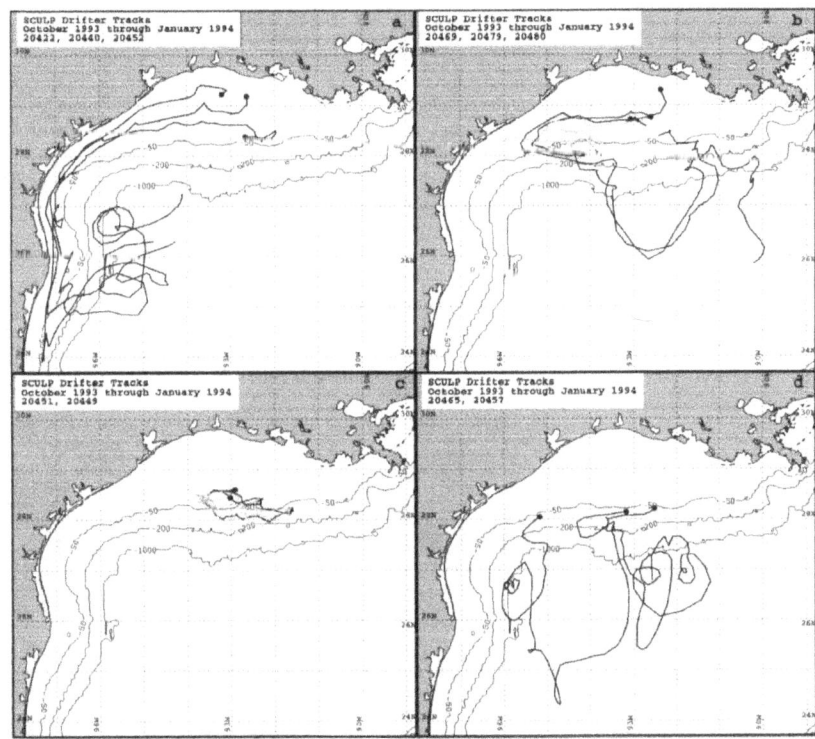

Figure 6. Tracks of selected SCULP drifters showing the main pathways during the 10/93 through 1/94: (a) Coastal current; (b) Matagorda squirt; (c) Mid-shelf cyclonic; and (d) Off-shelf eddy advection circulation.

It is interesting to note that wind reversals (from westward to eastward) associated with cold front passages notably altered the direction of movement of many of the drifters temporarily. This phenomenon is best observed in the drifter animation (Walter Johnson, Minerals Management Service, personal communication). Typically, the drifters reversed direction from a westward path to eastward path with the short-lived rotational wind regime of the winter storm event. However, when the wind regained a westward and southward component, current reversals occurred again rapidly and the down-coast flow within the coastal current regime once again prevailed.

The percentage of surface drifters that traveled down-coast within the coastal current to the Mexican shelf increased from 41% in October 1993 to 96% in January 1994 (Table 1). Daily averaged surface velocities were determined for the October and November drifters in this group. The average down-coast velocity between 94° W (along LA coast) and 26° N (along Texas/Mexican coast) was 20.2 cm/s (Figure 6a). Within this group, the fastest drifter traveled at an average daily speed of 38 cm/s and the slowest at 7 cm/s. The slower drifters generally exhibited more offshore/onshore movements and rotational motions resulting in the delayed travel time. During October and November 1993, approximately 60% of the coastal current group of drifters that made it to the Mexican shelf were advected seaward within an off-shelf flow (squirt) along the Mexican coast near 25.5° N. This squirt was formed between a warm core ring centered near 23.7° N and a cold core eddy north of it.

Table 1. Frequency (%) of main circulation patterns displayed by SCULP drifters from October 1993 through January 1994.

Circulation Pattern	10/93	11/93	12/93	1/94
1. Coastal Current (past 27° N)	41%	43%	70%	96%
2. Matagorda squirt (28°N)	41%	45%	30%	0%
3. LA shelf gyre	13%	0%	4%	0%
4. LA shelf to deep GOM (includes some Matagorda squirt drifters)	26%	32%	19%	4%
Mexican squirt (25.5° N, 23.5° N)	23%	27%	19%	16%
Groundings (Texas and Mexico)	0%	5%	11%	35%
No. of drifters in counts	39	44	27	26

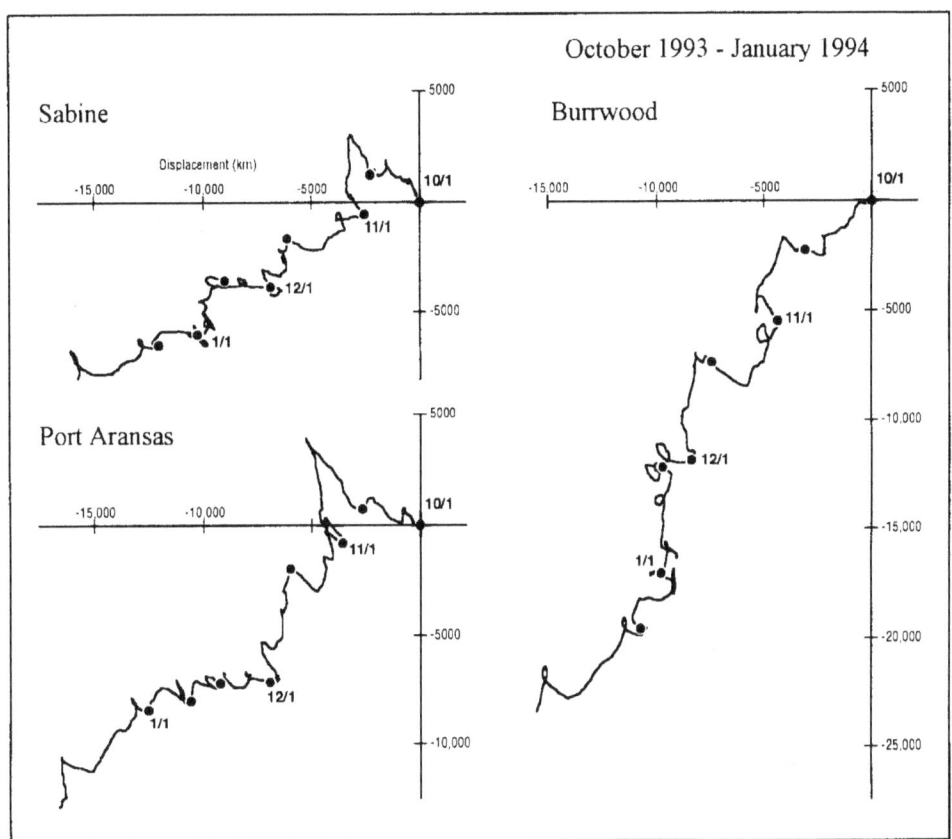

Figure 7. Progressive vector diagram of winds: October 1, 1993 through January 31, 1994 for Port Aransas, TX; Sabine, LA and Burrwood, LA. The vertical axis indicates north-south displacements with north as positive. The horizontal axis indicates east-west displacements with east as positive. The symbols depict day 1 and day 15 of each month. The Port Aransas data was missing October 1-7 and December 20, 1993- January 4, 1994.

The second main group of drifters initially traveled westward within the coastal current and then turned abruptly to the east/southeast within what appeared to be a well-defined narrow off-shelf jet that will be referred to as the Matagorda squirt (Figure 7b). The off-shelf flow in this region was more prevalent during October, November and early December 1993 when 30-45% of the drifters moved seaward in this region (Table 1). By January, this off-shelf flow feature may have disappeared as no drifters were observed to move seaward in that region. The satellite-derived SST and SSH data (Figure 5) indicated that the flow regime that resulted in the Matagorda squirt was closely associated with a well developed topographic high (anticyclonic circulation) of a warm core ring resident in the far northwest GOM. The SSH data also indicated a weak topographic low (cyclonic circulation) north of the warm core ring, a situation that could have enhanced off-shelf flow in this region during late October to mid-December 1993. Thus, this group of drifters moved eastward and southeastward between a warm core/cold core eddy pair. This narrow off-shelf jet was formed where the wind-driven inner and mid-shelf waters converged with the circulation associated with the CCE/WCE pair. The daily surface velocity averages (compiled using 4 drifters) were 39 cm/s in the Matagorda squirt with a range of 19-59 cm/s (Table 2). Many of the drifters that were advected seaward within the Matagorda squirt were then captured by strong southward surface currents on the east margin of the warm core ring in the northwest GOM. The surface velocities along the east side of the warm core ring in the far northwest GOM were slightly higher, averaging 45 cm/s with a range of 13-75 cm/s (Table 2). East of this ring, a cyclonic eddy and another (larger) warm core ring were present and their impacts on circulation are readily shown by the tracks of some of the drifters (Figure 5, 6b). A few of the drifters that were advected off-shelf in the Matagorda squirt remained on the shelf where they exhibited sluggish movement in a cyclonic circulation centered on the 50 m isobath (Figure 6c).

The second minor circulation pattern that was observed during the October 1993 to January 1994 period was a fairly direct flow from the Louisiana shelf seaward (Figure 6d). This pathway was exhibited primarily by drifters that were deployed in deeper water on the shelf.

The wind patterns were similar throughout the October 1993 through January1994 time period, therefore it is hypothesized that the change in circulation patterns shown in the drifter tracks was caused by a change in the location of warm and cold-core eddies/rings in the northwest GOM. The SST and SSH data provided evidence that the eddies that were initially close to the shelf moved away from the shelf during this time period. Thus, the drifters released in October and November 1993 were probably influenced to a greater degree by slope eddies due to their proximity to the Texas shelf edge than were those of December and January.

Table 2. Daily-average velocities of SCULP drifters affected by eddies and squirt features.

Drifter	Average daily velocity (cm/s)	Range of daily velocities (cm/s)
Matagorda squirt (Water depths > 50 and < 1000 m)		
20412	49	31-59
20480	26	19-38
20482	39	28-52
20469	41	36-51
	Mean 39	Range 19-59
Loop Current Ring (> 1000 m water depth, east side)		
20412	47	37-61
20480	56	43-65
20482	34	13-75
20469	44	41-48
	Mean 45	Range 13-75
Coastal current drifters advected into Mexican squirt		
20440	40	35-44
20407	32	15-51
20513	36	13-55
	Mean 36	Range 13-55

3. Surface Circulation Processes: Current Meter Analysis

Selected LATEX-A current meter measurements were investigated to yield a more quantitative understanding of shelf flow during the October to January period. Locations of the moorings to be discussed are shown in Figure 1. Inner shelf stations 2, 24, 21 and 18 were situated in 22-37 m of water and were chosen to represent flow within the Louisiana/Texas coastal current. The near-surface current meters were 8-14 m below the surface.

The current meter data have been represented graphically using progressive vector diagrams showing displacement in km (Figure 8) and in stick vector format (Figure 9). Wind vectors corresponding to the current vectors are shown in Figure 10. The progressive vector diagrams clearly revealed that the orientation of flow changed along the coast, in relation to the bathymetry. The net flow at mooring 21 was down-coast from October 1 to January 31 at an angle of approximately 265° (Figure 8). The net flow at mooring 24, further west, was down-coast at an angle of 242°, whereas at mooring 2 (further south), the down-coast flow was oriented more southward at an angle of 195-205° (Figure 8). At mooring 18, a partial record was obtained (from 12/6 to 1/31) indicating net flow to the west with a slight onshore component (Figure 8). At all of the mooring sites, flow was essentially parallel to the isobaths on the inner shelf. The down-coast velocities increased in the down-coast direction. Currents were stronger at moorings 2 and 24 along the Texas coastline than at moorings 18 and 21 further east on the Louisiana shelf (Figures 8,9; Tables 3,4). Strong coherence in the flow at moorings 2 and 24 was clearly evident from visual inspection of current vectors over the four months (Figure 9a-d). The periods of accelerated flow corresponded in time with strong southwestward wind stress (e.g. 10/21-10/27 and 11/6-11/11) (Figure 9a,b; 10a,b).

Current reversals occurred after major wind reversals associated with the west to east movement of winter storms through the study area. The strongest instantaneous currents were recorded at the southernmost station, mooring 2 (Figure 9) where a maximum velocity during the October to January period of 98 cm/s (Table 4) was recorded during a period of strong southward wind stress in early November 1993 (Figure 9b,10b). At mooring 24 the maximum current speed during the same event was 91 cm/s (Table 4). At mooring 21 the strongest down-coast currents in November were 43 cm/s but occurred during a southeast wind event, subsequent to the north wind event (Figure 9b, 10b). The strongest sustained velocities occurred at mooring 24 where maximum monthly velocities exceeded 70 cm/s during 7 months of the 11 months analyzed (Table 4). Maximum monthly velocities at mooring 2 exceeded 60 cm/s during 6 months. Acceleration of the coastal current was related to acceleration in the alongshore wind stress, as suggested by Cochrane and Kelly (1986) and Murray (1998). Current velocities were noticeably stronger during two periods of the October to January record: October 21 to November 17, 1993 and January 9 to 22, 1994 time periods that exhibited strong southwestward wind stress. During both periods, the net flow was in the down-coast (westward) direction. During the four month period, the net down-coast displacement at mooring 24 was 2300 km compared with 1400 km at mooring 2 (Figure 7) and 1000 km at mooring 21. The mean and maximum velocities for these four moorings are given in Tables 3 and 4.

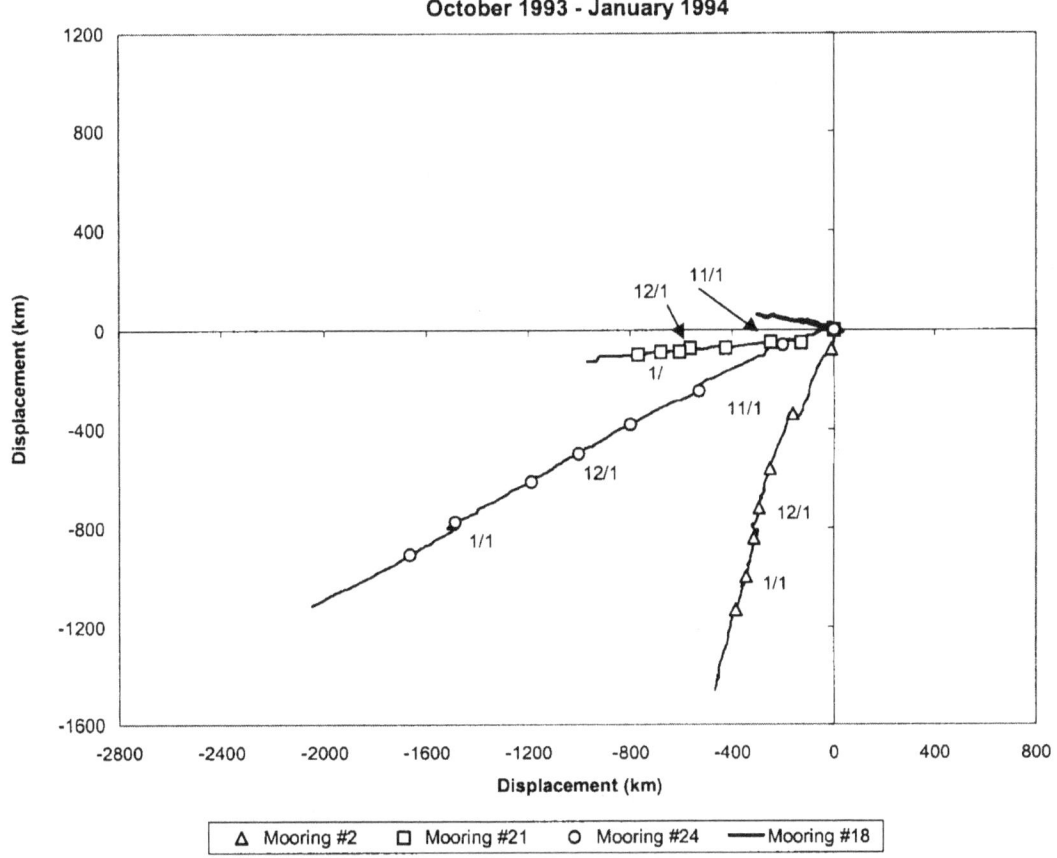

Figure 8. Progressive vector diagram of currents: October 1, 1993 - January 31, 1994 for LATEX moorings 2, 24, 21 (Locations in Figure 1). The mooring 18 data were available from December 6 - January 31. Days 1 and 15 are indicated with symbols. The vertical axis shows north-south displacement with north positive. The horizontal axis shows east-west displacement with east positive.

Mooring 7 was located along the 200 m isobath, in close proximity to the narrow Matagorda squirt circulation feature (Location, Figure 1). Current meter data were available from this station beginning on December 11, 1993. The record demonstrates persistent flow to the east (northeast and southeast) from December 11 through January 19, 1994 (Figure 11). After that time, the most prevalent flow regime was northwestward and southwestward through March 1994 (not shown). This record ties in with the drifter analyses that showed that the last drifter to exit the shelf via the Matagorda squirt was deployed in late December 1993. Most of the drifters deployed in January 1994 remained on the shelf within the coastal current, crossing the U.S./Mexican border at 26°N. A comparison of satellite altimetry contours for November 28, 1993 and December 14, 1993 demonstrate that the warm core ring in the northwest GOM moved southeastward over that 16 day period (Figure 12). It is likely that the seaward movement of the warm core ring removed the advection mechanism set-up between the anticyclonic ring and cyclonic eddy situated north of it.

19

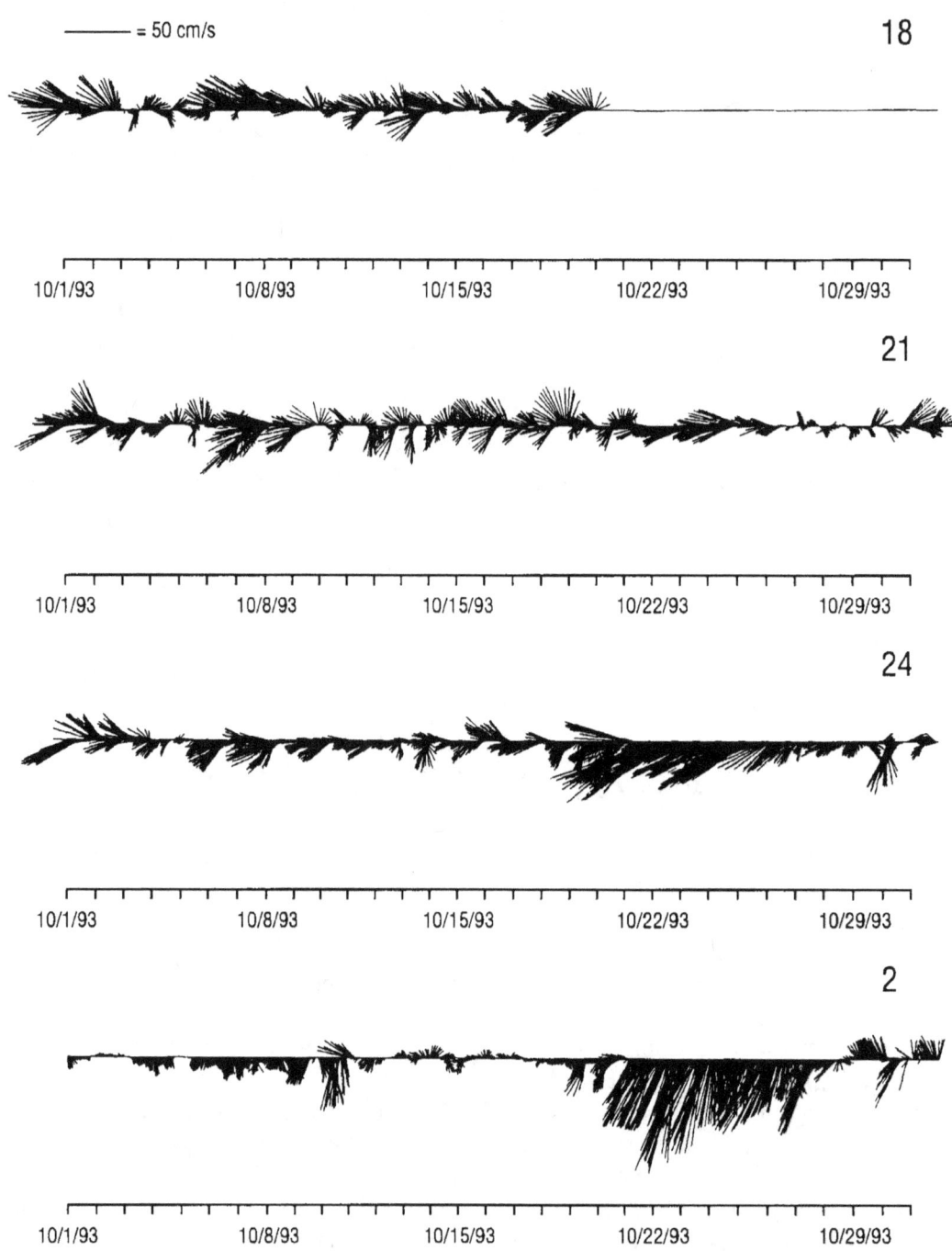

Figure 9. Stick vector representation of current meter data for moorings 18, 21, 24 and 2 for **(a) October 1993**; (b) November 1993; (c) December 1993; and (d) January 1994. Standard oceanographic vector orientation is used. Northward currents point to top of page.

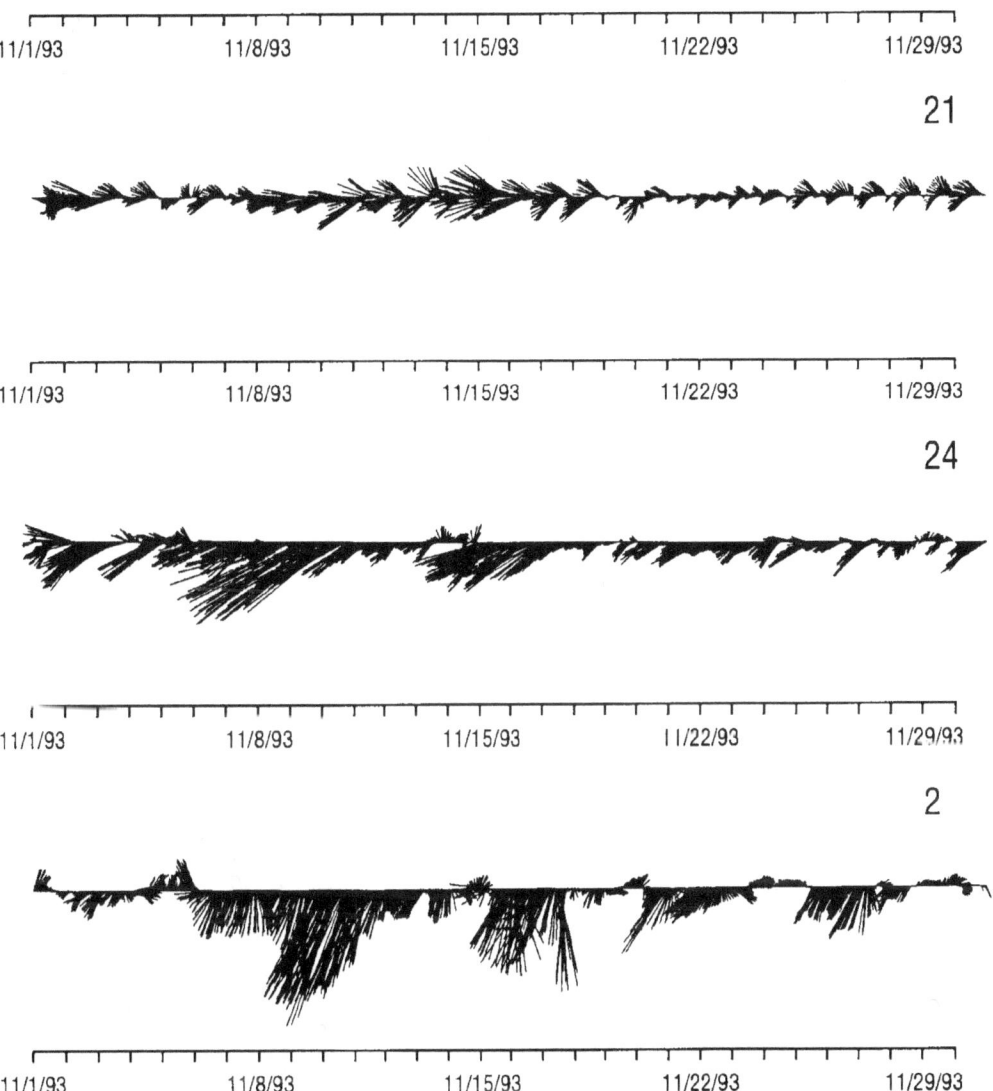

= 50 cm/s

18

11/1/93   11/8/93   11/15/93   11/22/93   11/29/93

21

11/1/93   11/8/93   11/15/93   11/22/93   11/29/93

24

11/1/93   11/8/93   11/15/93   I I/22/93   11/29/93

2

11/1/93   11/8/93   11/15/93   11/22/93   11/29/93

Figure 9 (continued). Stick vector representation of current meter data for moorings 18, 21, 24 and 2 for (a) October 1993; **(b) November 1993**; (c) December 1993; and (d) January 1994. Standard oceanographic vector orientation is used. Northward currents point to top of page.

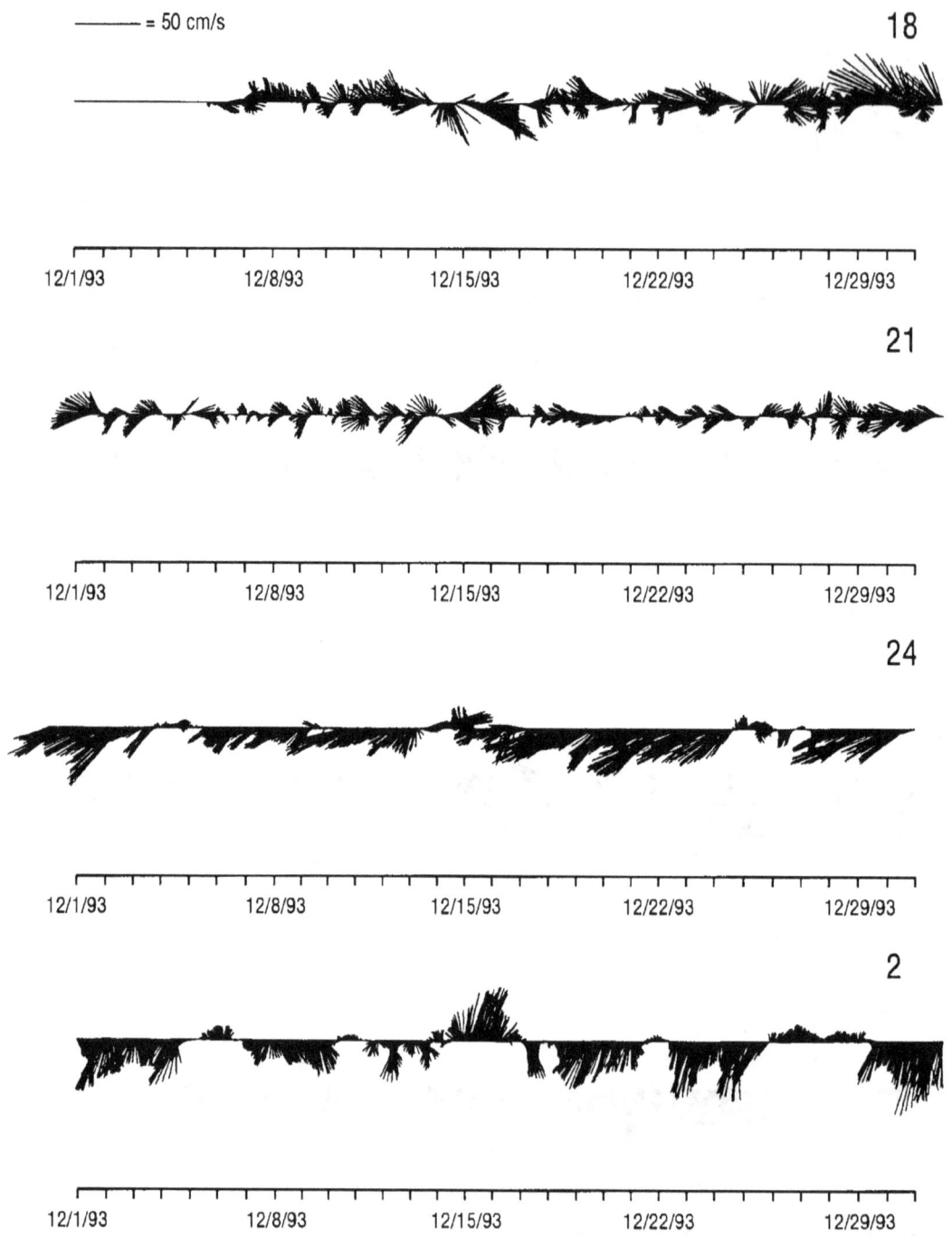

Figure 9 (continued). Stick vector representation of current meter data for moorings 18, 21, 24 and 2 for (a) October 1993; (b) November 1993; **(c) December 1993**; and (d) January 1994. Standard oceanographic vector orientation is used. Northward currents point to top of page.

22

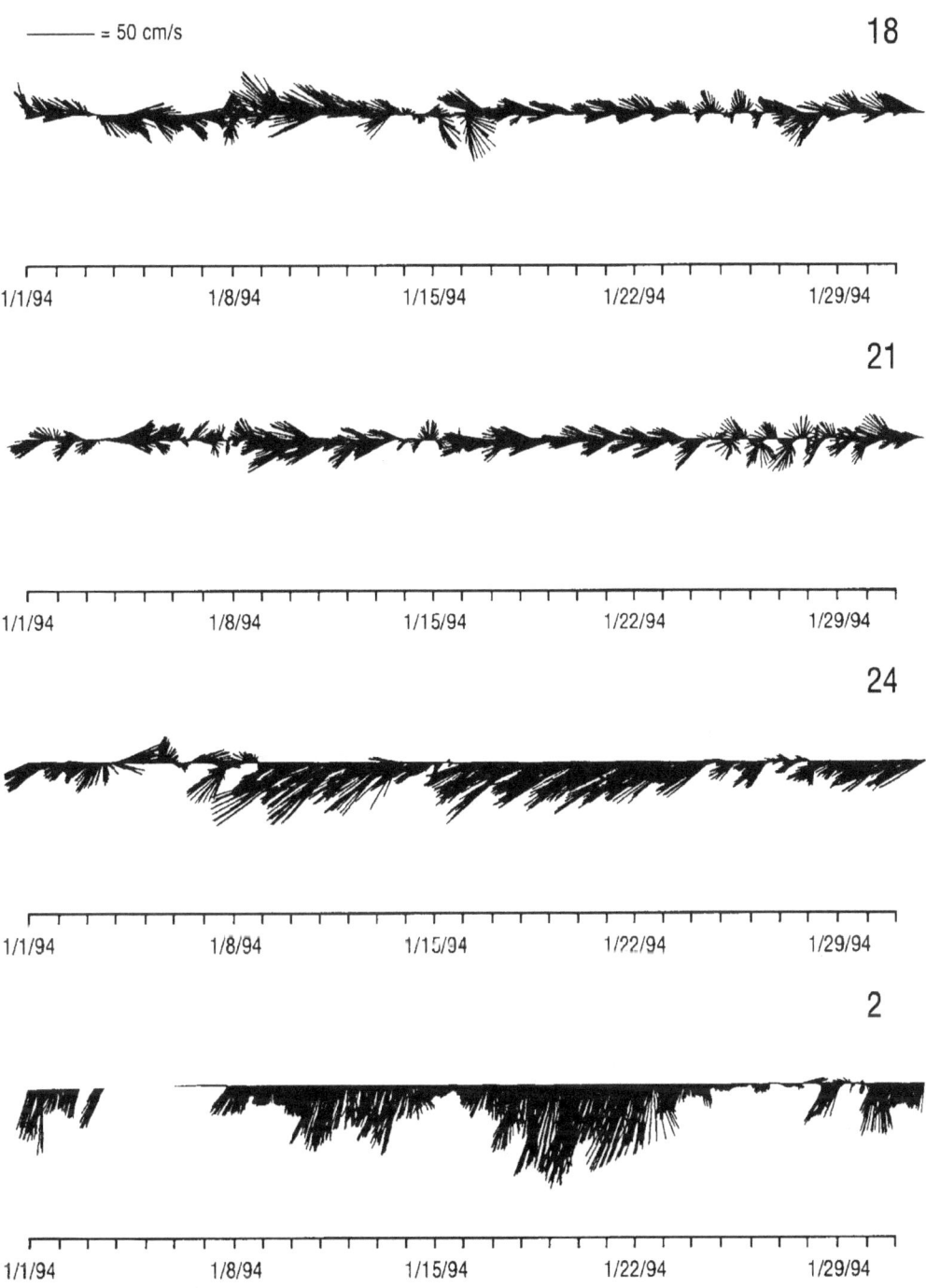

Figure 9 (continued). Stick vector representation of current meter data for moorings 18, 21, 24 and 2 for (a) October 1993; (b) November 1993; (c) December 1993; and **(d) January 1994**. Standard oceanographic vector orientation is used. Northward currents point to top of page.

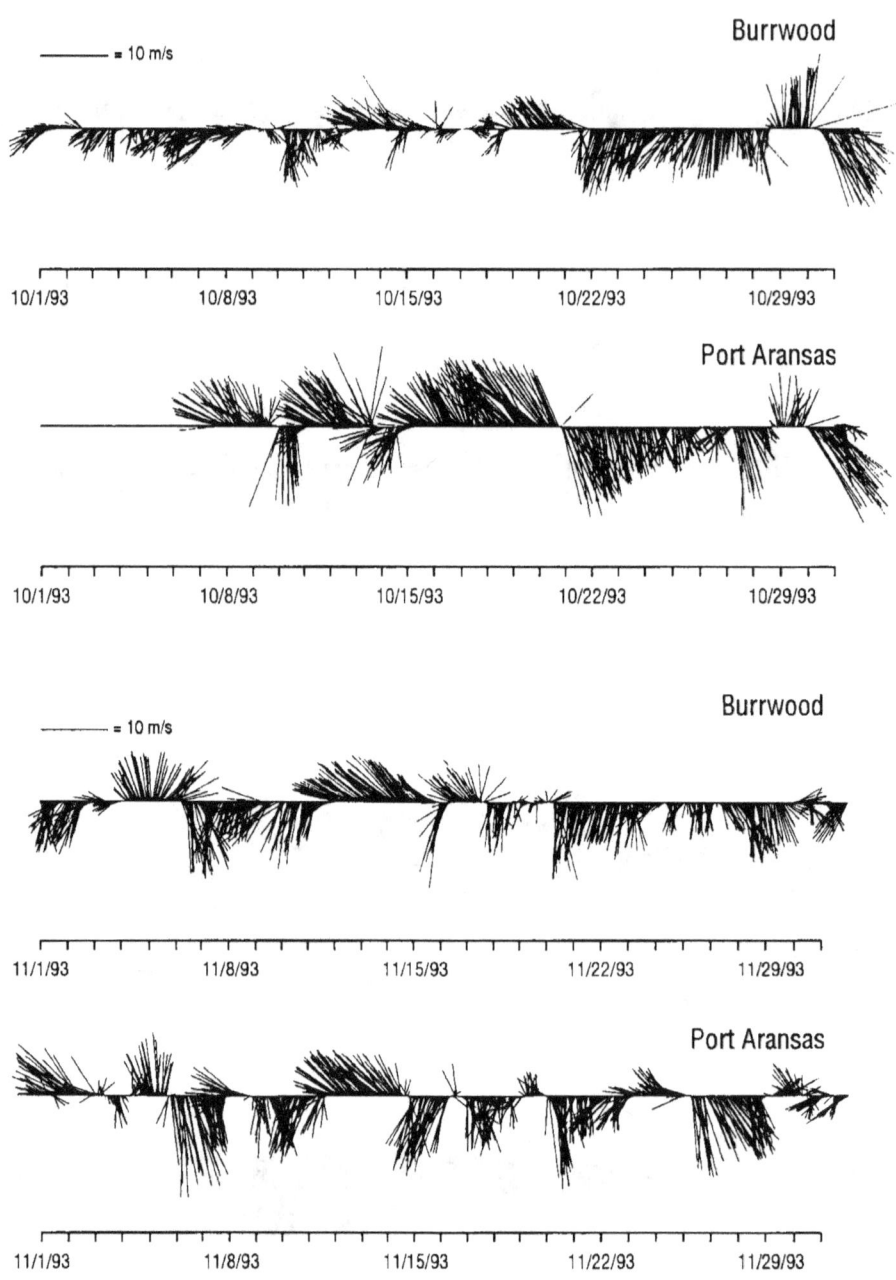

Figure 10. Stick vector representation of wind speed and direction data from Burrwood, LA and Port Aransas, TX for **(a) October 1993**; **(b) November 1993**; (c) December 1993 and (d) January 1994. Oceanographic vector orientation is used where winds blowing to the north point to the top of the page.

24

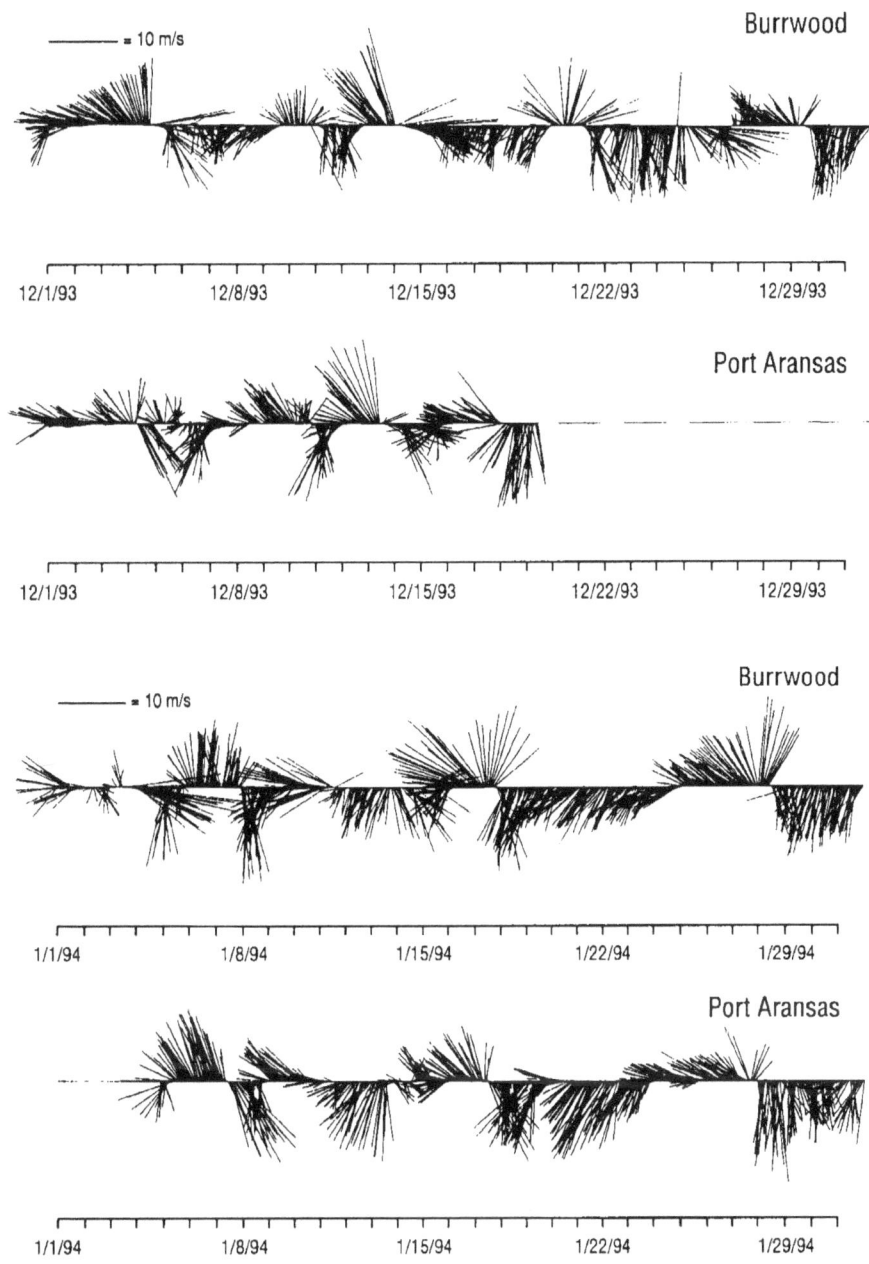

Figure 10. Stick vector representation of wind speed and direction data from Burrwood, LA and Port Aransas, TX for (a) October 1993; (b) November 1993; **(c) December 1993** and **(d) January 1994**. Oceanographic vector orientation is used where winds blowing to the north point to the top of the page.

Table 3. Monthly-averaged current velocities (cm/s) for selected LATEX-A moorings (see figure 1 for locations).

Month	Moorings				
	2	24	21	18	7
Oct-93	17.97	24.77	16.72	17.52	
Nov-93	20.35	22.03	14.45		
Dec-93	17.17	24.94	11.97	17.26	11.91
Jan-94	24.24	28.58	17.12	17.62	20.63
Feb-94	15.49	22.85	12.00	05.04	15.13
Mar-94	15.30	19.17	11.78	16.18	12.80
Apr-94	19.80	19.66	17.72	18.77	14.45
May-94	17.81	26.60	12.15	10.36	17.31
Jun-94	23.21	22.94	18.09	14.21	17.95
Jul-94	10.55	19.49	17.22	18.29	23.04
Aug-94	12.38	14.37	10.60	12.02	15.87
Mean	17.66	22.31	14.53	14.73	16.57

Table 4. Monthly-maxima of current velocities (cm/s) for selected LATEX-A moorings (see figure 1 for locations).

Month	Moorings				
	2	24	21	18	7
Oct-93	87.70	84.4	55.80	53.60	
Nov-93	98.00	90.9	43.00		
Dec-93	57.00	71.8	39.70	62.00	40.70
Jan-94	76.60	80.4	48.00	43.20	69.80
Feb-94	54.80	67.3	38.20	27.00	38.20
Mar-94	69.30	72.8	39.70	50.90	27.40
Apr-94	55.60	70.7	55.30	62.00	44.40
May-94	64.50	72.5	29.90	40.80	41.90
Jun-94	60.00	77.4	40.80	35.90	72.10
Jul-94	33.70	57	44.60	70.50	59.50
Aug-94	39.30	45.3	26.10	33.60	46.80

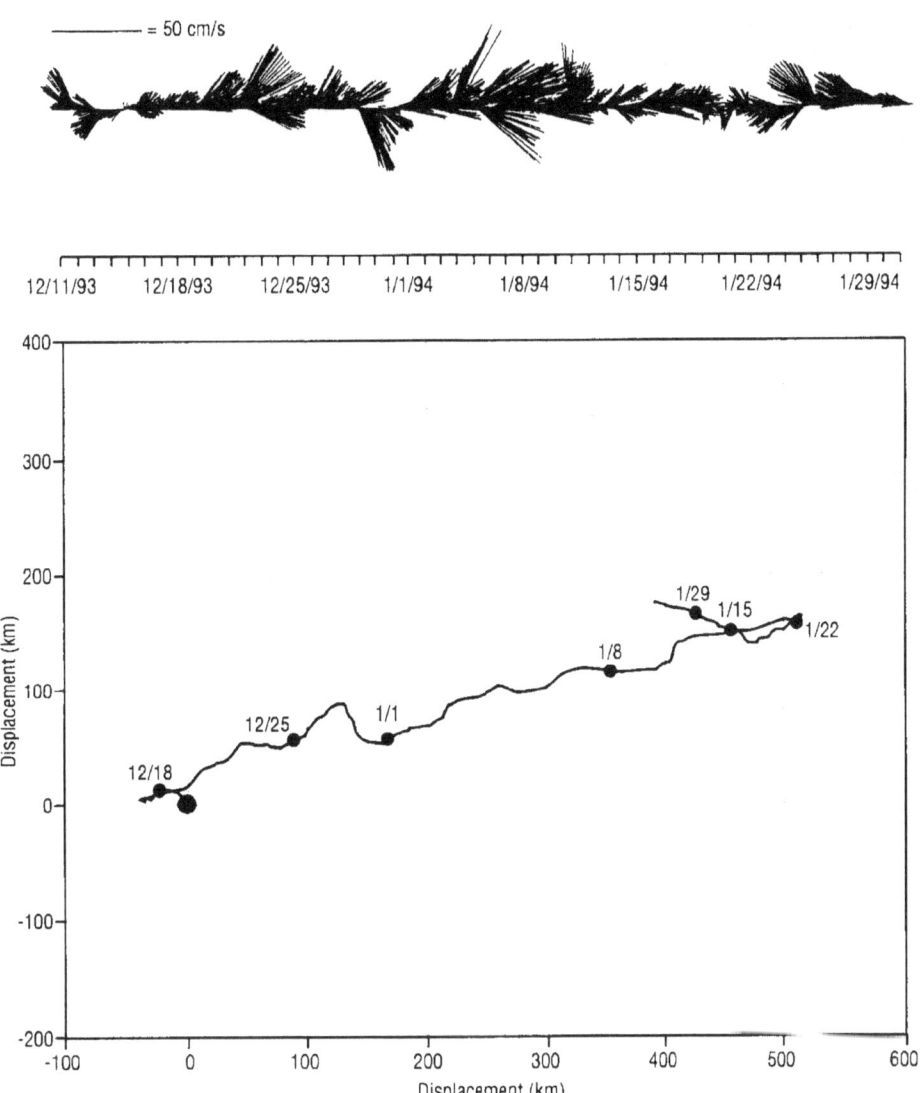

Figure 11. Mooring 7 current meter data plotted as stick vectors (top panel). Standard oceanographic vector orientation is used where northward currents point to top of page. Mooring 7 current displacement (bottom panel) for December 11, 1993 through January 31, 1994. Symbols are plotted every 7 days. The vertical axis shows north-south displacements, with north positive. The horizontal axis shows east-west displacements, with east positive.

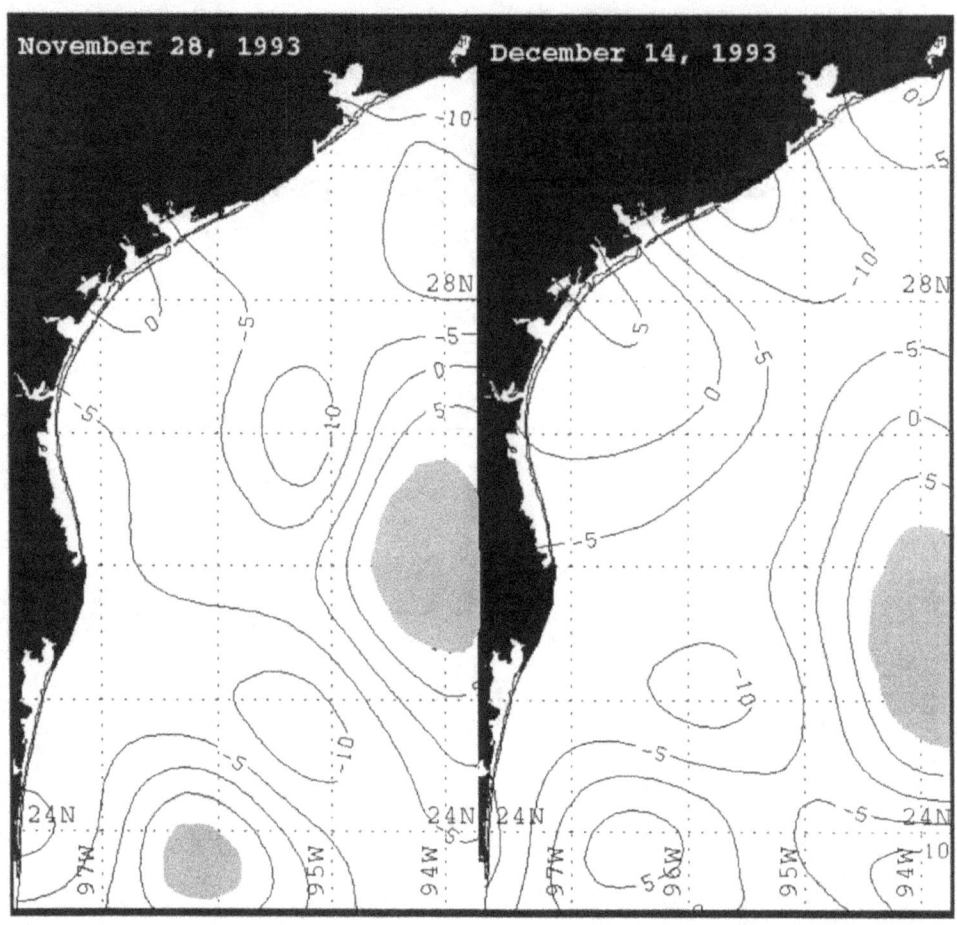

Figure 12. SSH anomaly contour maps for the northwest GOM on November 28, 1993 and December 14, 1993 (courtesy of Dr. Bob Leben, CCAR, Boulder, Colorado). Positive height anomalies exceeding 10 cm are shaded.

The SSH analysis of December 14, 1993(Figure 12) revealed a warm core ring near 24° N and 96° W and a cold core ring just north of it. These features were confirmed by SST patterns and by drifter movements. A sequence of clear-sky satellite images (Dec. 5/6 through January 8, 1994) enabled the study of the movement of eddy features along the shelf and the development and evolution of a high-velocity off-shelf flow feature, a Mexican squirt. A schematic of the six clearest images over the month period are shown in Figure 13 and three of the satellite images are shown in Figure 14. This image sequence clearly revealed that there was a northward

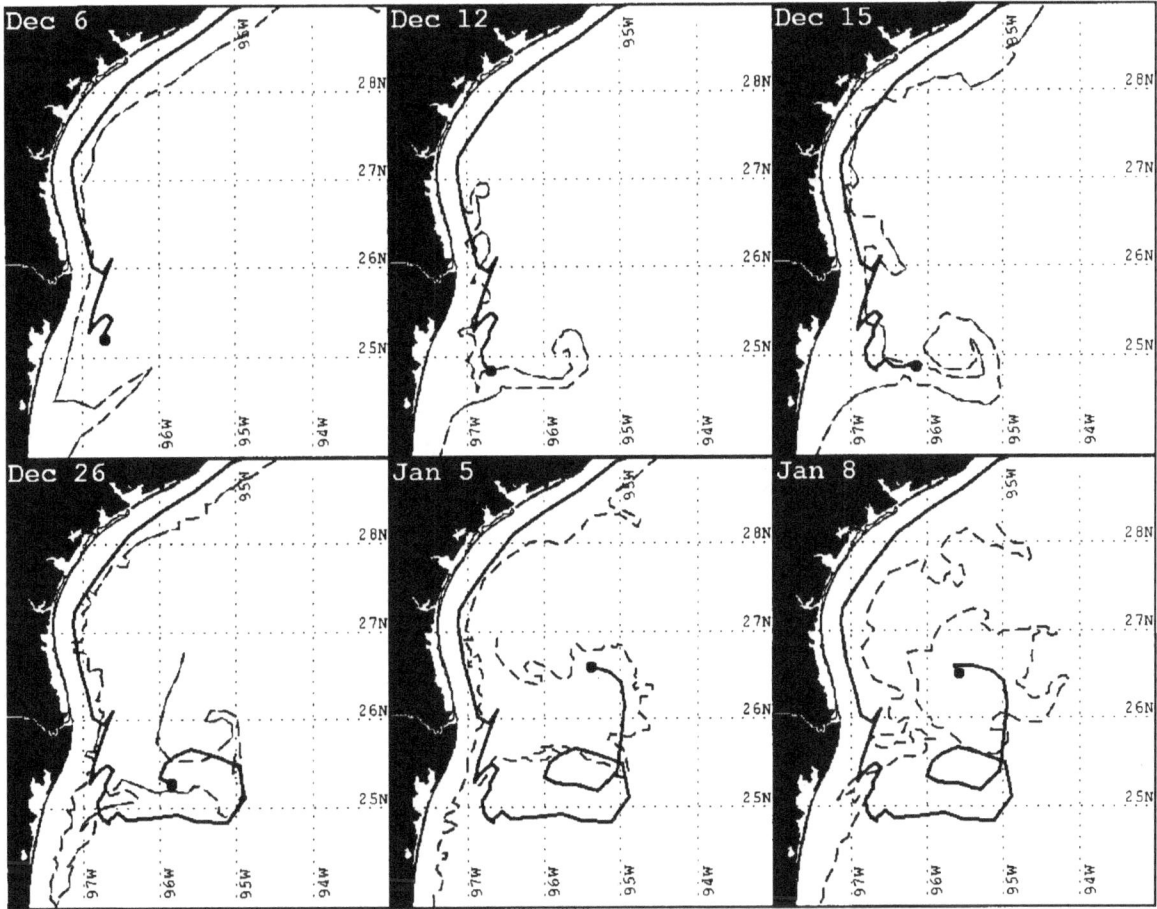

Figure 13. Schematic representation of the formation, evolution and spin-down phase of a Mexican squirt from December 6, 1993 through January 8, 1994 as observed in satellite SST data. The track of a SCULP drifter is superimposed on the imagery with the filled circle marking its position at the time of image acquisition.

movement of eddies close to the shelf edge between 25° and 27° between December 14, 1993 and January 8, 1994. This movement coincided in time with the southeast movement of the warm core ring in the northwest GOM.

This image sequence also depicted the offshelf advection of a large mass of cool shelf water associated with a warm core/cold core eddy pair along the Mexican coast. On December 5/6 the initial phase of significant offshelf advection was noted in the satellite SST data (Figure 12a; Figure 13a). This feature "grew" in the seaward direction rather rapidly. On December 5/6, the seaward extent of the feature was detected near 96°W. By December 12, the seaward extent of the cool water was at 95.5°W and by December 15, the feature extended to 95°W. Between December 15 and December 26, the feature moved primarily northwards. By January 4/5, a large almost circular body of cool shelf water measuring about 20,000 km^2 in area was apparent in the satellite imagery. On January 8, the cool water body had severed its connection from the shelf water.

Many of the coastal current drifters released on the Louisiana shelf in late October and November 1993 moved offshore along the Mexican coastline in this squirt feature. Daily averaged surface velocities (determined from 3 drifters) within the squirt were 36 cm/s with a daily range of 13-55 cm/s (Table 2). The drifter movements showed the presence of two relatively small-scale cyclonic circulation features north of this squirt. The diameters of the drifter tracks within the cyclonic eddies (Figure 6) were 94 x 50 km and 98 x 69 km.

B. Summer Season Circulation Processes

1. Winter to Summer Sea Surface Warming

The coldest winter temperatures usually occur along the Louisiana and Texas coasts in January when minima of 14° C are common (Figure 2). Warming of coastal waters proceeds rapidly from February to May when climatological temperature increases of 10-12° C are experienced. To investigate the behavior of regional warming on the Louisiana/Texas shelf, satellite-derived SST data were extracted from three relatively clear sky image: January 4, 1994, April 24, 1994 and June 28, 1994. Along profile lines D and E, dates in July were substituted as June 28 was excessively cloudy in these regions.

The satellite image composite of April 24/7 is shown in Figure 15 with the location of the profile lines. The imagery revealed that surface shelf waters were almost isothermal across the region ranging from 22-25° C. The cool coastal waters and the intense surface fronts observed in winter were not observed in this April image. The coolest waters were Mississippi and Atchafalaya River waters entering the GOM. However, the river waters warmed rapidly on the inner shelf and Louisiana shelf waters were 1-2° C warmer compared with Texas. This may have resulted from greater stratification on the Louisiana shelf due to the prevalence of relatively fresh river water. This stratification would have reduced the depth of the mixed layer and, thus, have increased the rapidity of surface warming. From January 4 to April 24, surface temperatures increased 4 to 12° C along the inner shelf (Figure 16) with the largest changes occurring close to the coast. Along line A on the south Texas shelf, surface temperatures of 21.5-22.5° C were measured. Since January 4, warming of 4-5 ° C had occurred on the inner shelf, but a slight cooling (0.5-1° C) had occurred on the middle and outer shelf regions. Along Line B, temperatures ranged from 22-23° C across the shelf, demonstrating a 4-8° C increase on the inner shelf and almost no change seaward of 60 km. The temperatures along lines C, D and E on April 24, 1994, ranged from 21-25° C (Figure 16). Between the January and April images, inner shelf waters had warmed 10-12° C whereas outer shelf waters had only warmed 1-3° C. Along line F, near the Mississippi Delta, warming was similar across the shelf. Note that cloud contamination lowered surface temperatures along line F on January 4, 1994 in the outer shelf region. Along line E, cloud cover effected SST retrieval between 90 and 105 km from the coast on April 24.

Surface temperatures extracted from the June 28, 1994 image showed warming of 5-8 °C on most of the shelf over the intervening two month period. Similar temperature change was also measured at LATEX moorings 18 and 21 at mid-depth (12-14 m from water surface). Along the coast of Texas (and Mexico), however, a different situation was encountered as a distinct band of cool waters extended from 23° N to 29.5° N (Figure 16, Figure 17). These relatively cool waters resulted from wind-forced upwelling along the coast and were readily detectable along line A (Figure 16) where cool waters near 25° C extended out from the coast at least 20 km. Relatively cool waters (26-27° C) were also observed along profile line B (Figure 16) extending 30 km from the coast. There was no evidence of upwelling along lines C, D, or E (Figures 16, 17). Cool coastal waters were also detected in the satellite imagery south along the Mexican coast to at least 23° N (Figure 17).

Along lines D and E (Figures 16), cloud-cover prohibited the extraction of surface temperatures on June 28 and, therefore, temperatures were extracted from imagery of July 3 and July 26. The imagery demonstrated that temperatures on the Louisiana shelf were fairly uniform, ranging from 28-30° C on June 28 and warming to 30-33 ° C by July along lines E and F (Figure 16). The warmest shelf waters were detected between the plumes of the two rivers. Based on the climatological data for Grand Isle (Figure 2), the warmest coastal temperatures would be expected during the months of July and August.

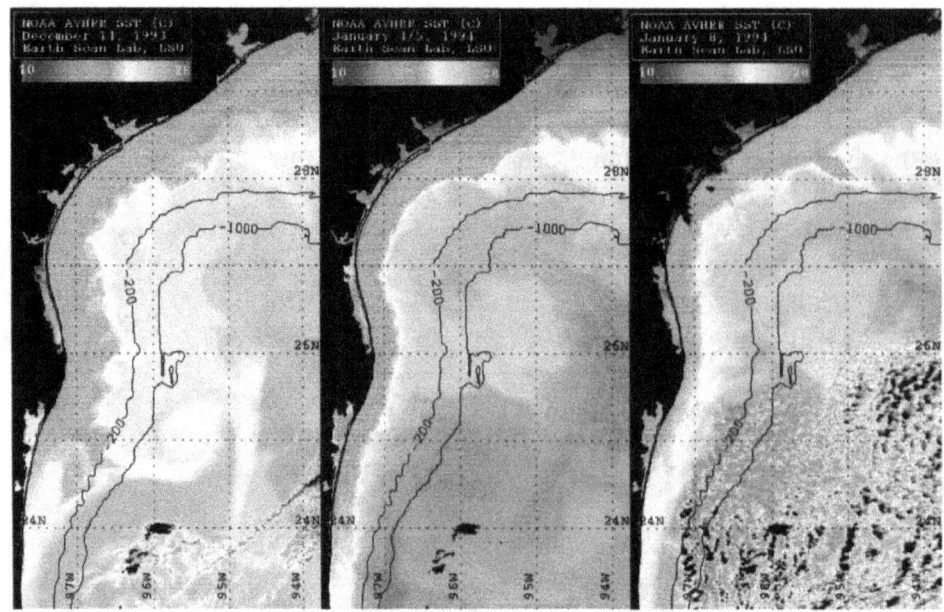

Figure 14. Sequence of three SST satellite images: December 14, 1993; January 4/5, 1994 and January 8, 1994 depicting the offshore entrainment of cold shelf water (Mexican squirt) by warm/cold core eddy pair near 25° N latitude and the subsequent evolution of this feature with ultimate separation from shelf waters and movement eastward over the slope.

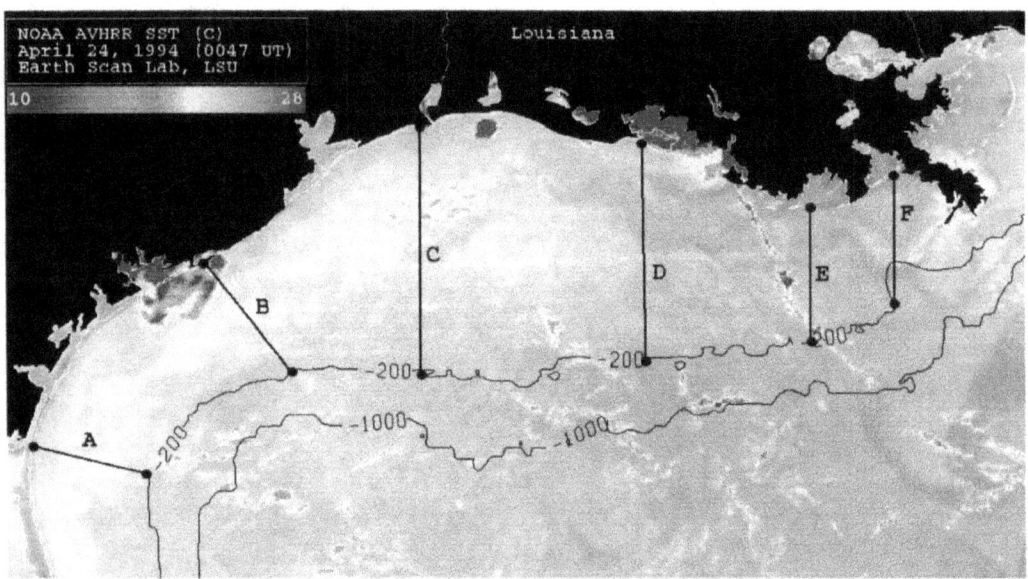

Figure 15. NOAA AVHRR SST image of April 24, 1994 (0047 UTC) enhanced with the same color table as Figures 3 and 13. The locations of the profile lines from which surface temperatures were extracted are shown. A large cloud mass was encountered in the Matagorda Bay region (purple color on imagery).

2. Surface Circulation: Current Meter Analyses

The regional wind measurements, shown in progressive vector format (Figure 18), demonstrated that dramatic changes in the wind direction were experienced between autumn/winter 1993/94 and spring/summer 1994. Northward winds became more frequent and stronger along the Texas and Louisiana coast during May, June and July 1994. The strongest northward winds occurred in June and July. During these months, winds blew towards the northwest along the southern Texas coastline (at Port Aransas) and towards the north along the Louisiana coast (Sabine and Burrwood). The Sabine station record is included as it adds important information on spatial variability of the wind, however, the reader is cautioned that the record at this station was missing one week in May 1994 and 4 weeks in June 1994.

This major change in the prevailing wind direction during summer caused a reversal of flow of the Louisiana/Texas coastal current. The progressive vector diagram of currents (Figure 19) for moorings 2, 24, 21 and 18 indicated that up-coast flow (northward and eastward currents) dominated near surface circulation during June and July. Figure 9 demonstrated that flow at each station essentially reversed direction by about 180°, thus up-coast flow paralleled the isobaths as did the down-coast flow in winter. A more detailed comparison of the current meter records (Figure 20) for May, June and July revealed that weak current reversals (down-coast to up-coast) occurred at mooring 2 during May, but it was not until June 8 that the up-coast flow became well

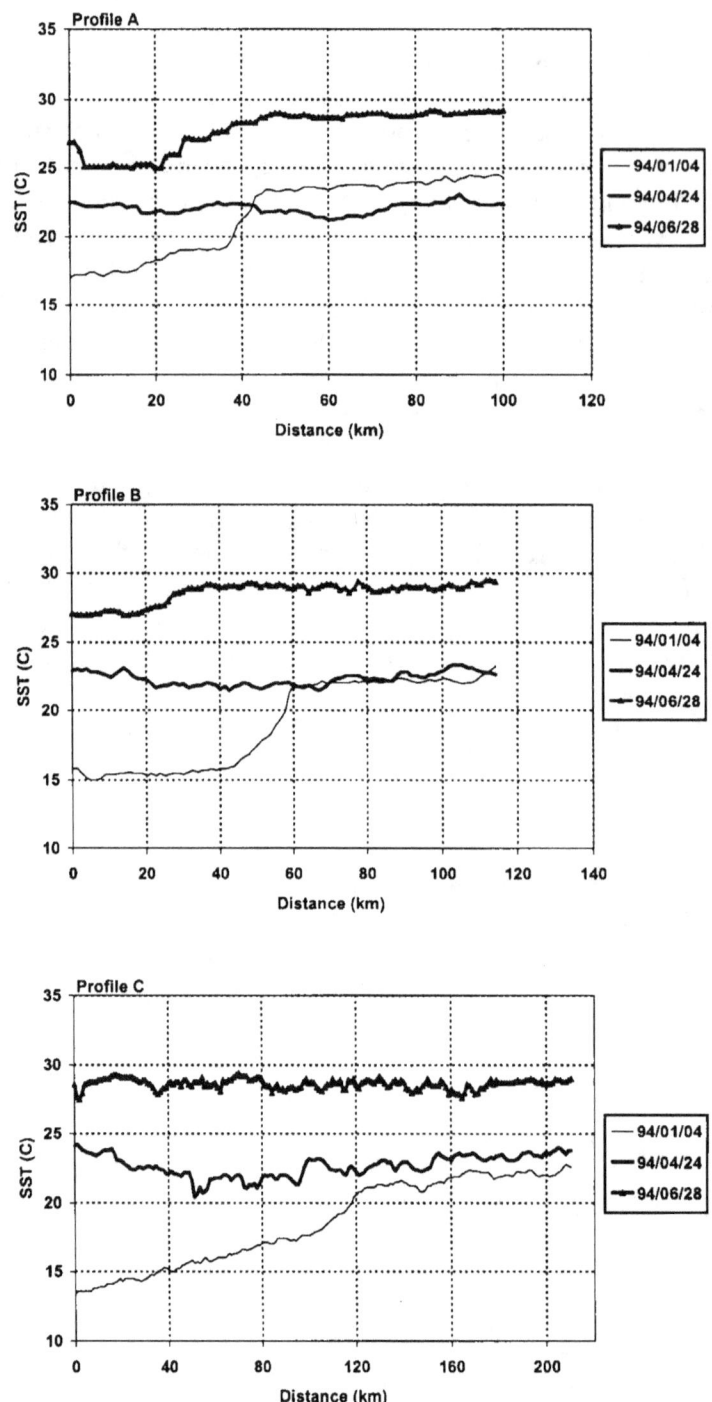

Figure 16. SST data extracted from 6 profile lines (A-F) on January 4, 1994; April 24, 1994 and June 28, 1994 (Locations, Figure 15). Due to cloud cover on June 28, image data obtained on July 3 and 26, 1994 were substituted for lines E and F.

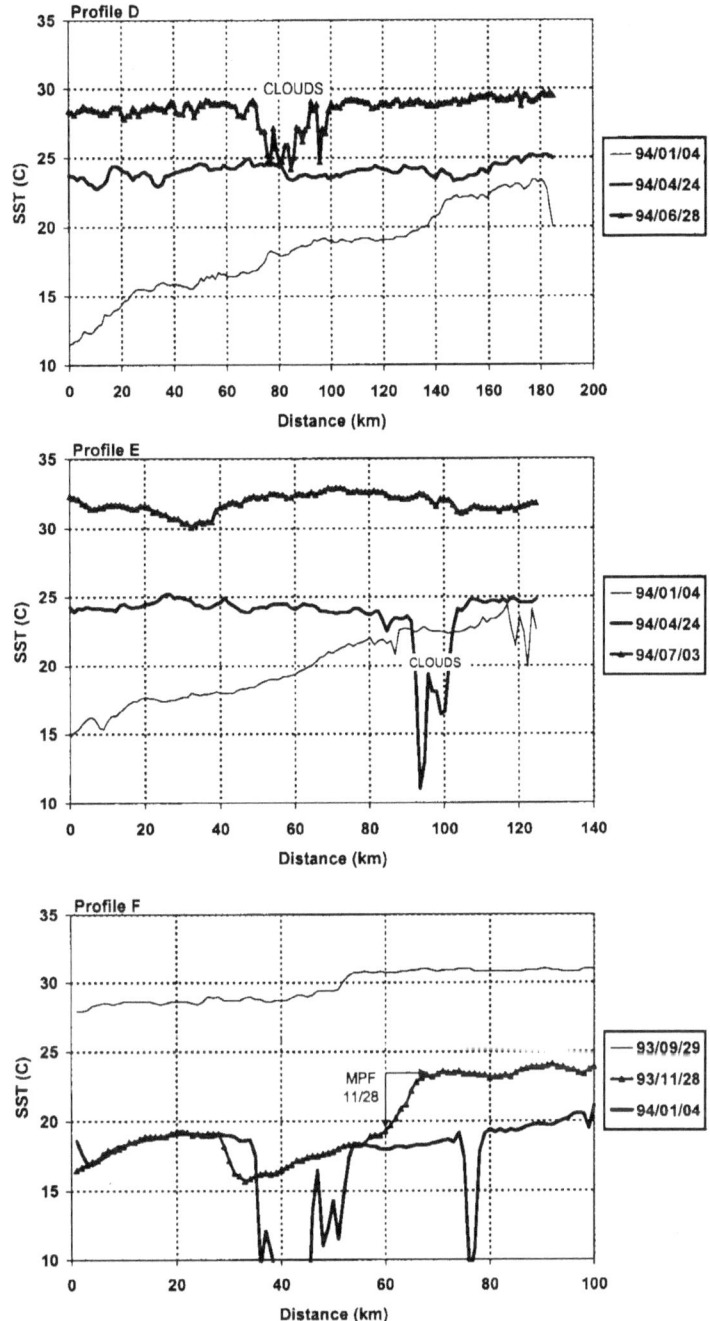

Figure 16 (continued). SST data extracted from 6 profile lines (A-F) on January 4, 1994; April 24, 1994 and June 28, 1994 (Locations, Figure 15). Due to cloud cover on June 28, image data obtained on July 3 and 26, 1994 were substituted for lincs E and F. MPF refers to Mississippi plume front.

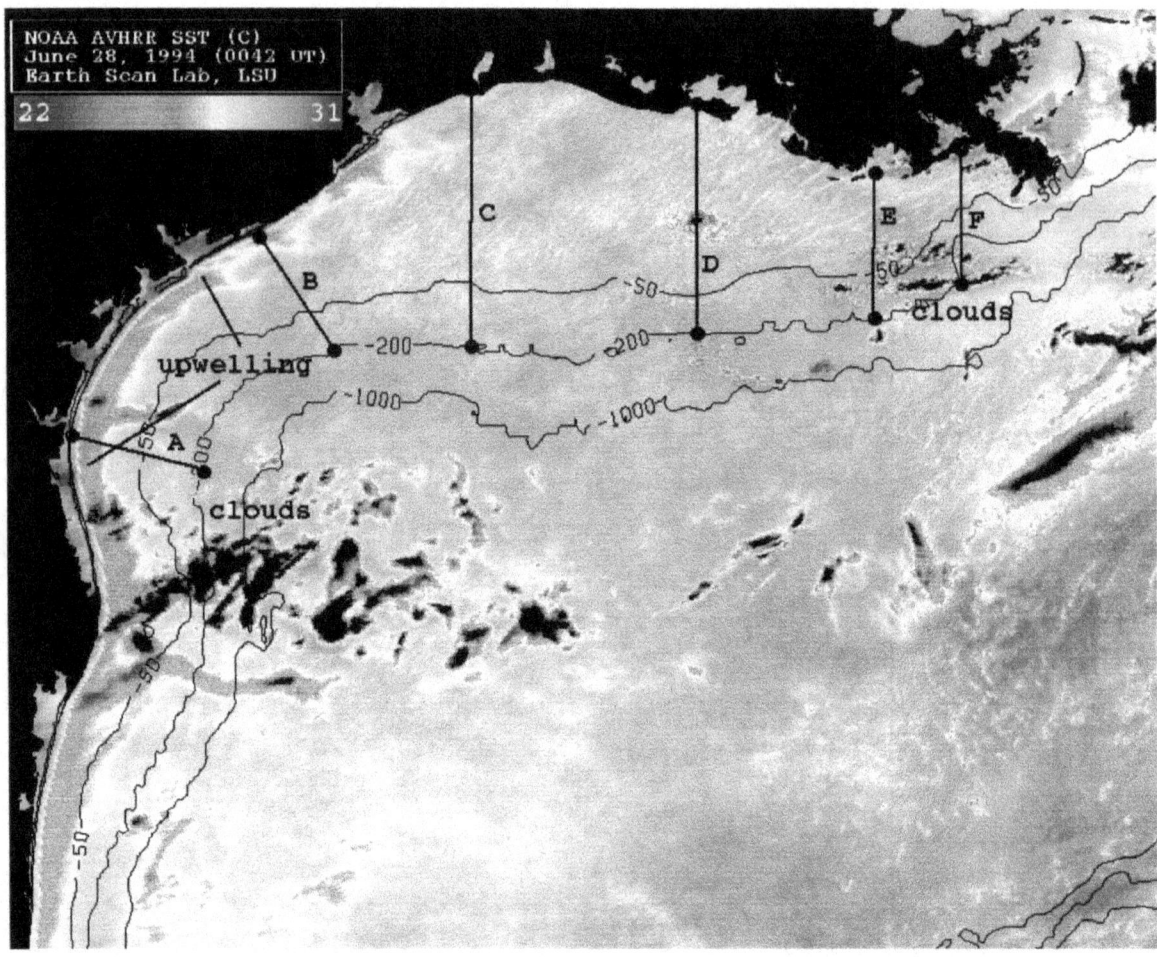

Figure 17. NOAA AVHRR SST image obtained on June 28, 1994 (0042 UTC). Upwelled water along the coast of Texas is depicted with blue and green colors. The locations of the profile lines are indicated.

established. The current reversal at mooring 2 on June 8 lagged the onset of northward wind stress by several weeks. The top meter at mooring 2 was located 8-10 m below the surface.

The initiation of the up-coast flow regime of summer across the region was of particular interest. A distinct and prolonged current reversal, from down-coast to up-coast flow, first occurred at mooring 21 (south of Sabine). The shift to northward wind stress at Sabine preceded the other meteorological stations. From June 1-7, strong northward wind stress (Figure 21) resulted in strong onshore flow at mooring 21 (Figure 20). During this period, the flow at mooring 24, further south remained down-coast. In contrast, currents at mooring 18 along the Louisiana inner shelf were eastward (Figure 20). It is postulated that the northward winds elevated water levels in the Sabine/Galveston region producing a pressure gradient that resulted in flow away from this region, to the east along LA coast and to the south along the TX coast. After about 1 week, up-coast flow prevailed at the top moorings (8-10 m) on the inner shelf from

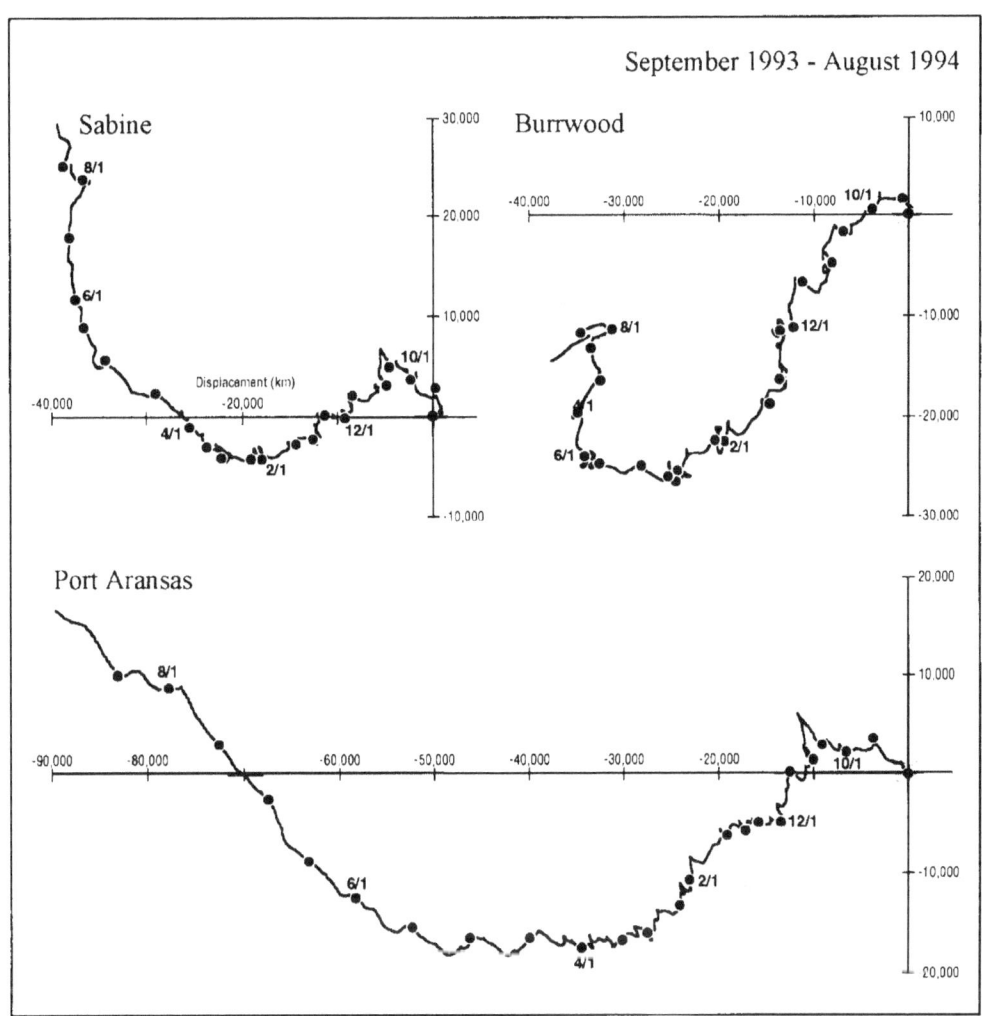

Figure 18. Progressive vector diagrams of wind speed and direction from September 1, 1993 through August 31, 1994 for the C-MAN stations of Burrwood, LA; Sabine, LA and Port Aransas, TX. Symbols mark days 1 and 15 of each month. Data were unavailable at the Sabine station for 1 week in May and all of June 1994. Port Aransas was missing 7 days in October, 11 days in December and 3 days in January. The vertical axis depicts north-south directions with north positive. The horizontal axis depicts east-west direction with east positive.

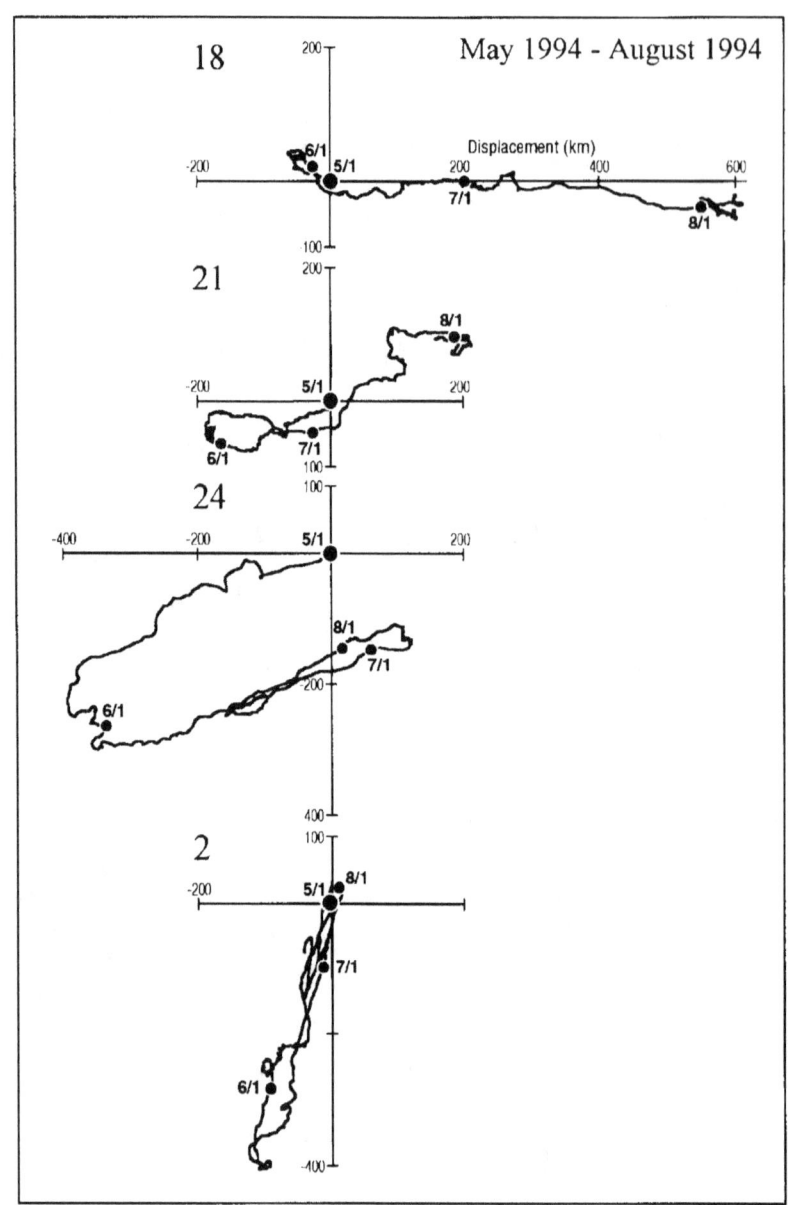

Figure 19. Progressive vector diagrams of current speed and direction from May 1, 1994 through August 31, 1994 for LATEX moorings 18, 21, 24 and 2. The symbols indicate day 1 of each month. The vertical axis depicts north-south directions with north as positive. The horizontal axis depicts east-west direction with east positive.

south Texas to Louisiana (Figure 20). During the summer period, the strongest up-coast flow occurred along the Texas inner shelf between June 23 and June 30, corresponding in time to the strongest regional northward wind stress (Figure 21). In contrast, the strongest up-coast flow at mooring 18 occurred when wind stress switched from northward to northeastward, increasing the alongshore component to the east.

The drifter data (representative of flow within the top few meters) showed an almost immediate response of the currents to changes in wind direction. For examples, current reversals were observed in the drifter data on May 22-24 (drifters 21710, 21702) and on June 21 (drifter 21736) (not shown) coincident with major wind shifts from south to north (Figure 21).

These two sources of current information revealed that up-coast surface flow along the southern Texas coast was driven primarily by the northward wind stress, however, the currents at 8-10 m water depth along the southern Texas coast lagged the wind stress by a few weeks. Once the up-coast flow regime was established, however, velocities were enhanced by an increase in northward wind stress. Along the Louisiana coast, the along-shore eastward flow was maximized during conditions of strong eastward wind stress. The currents at mooring 21 were more complex, ranging from northward to eastward flow during June and July 1994. When up-coast flow along the south Texas coast was well established (such as from June 23-30), currents at mooring 21 were predominantly eastward rather than northward.

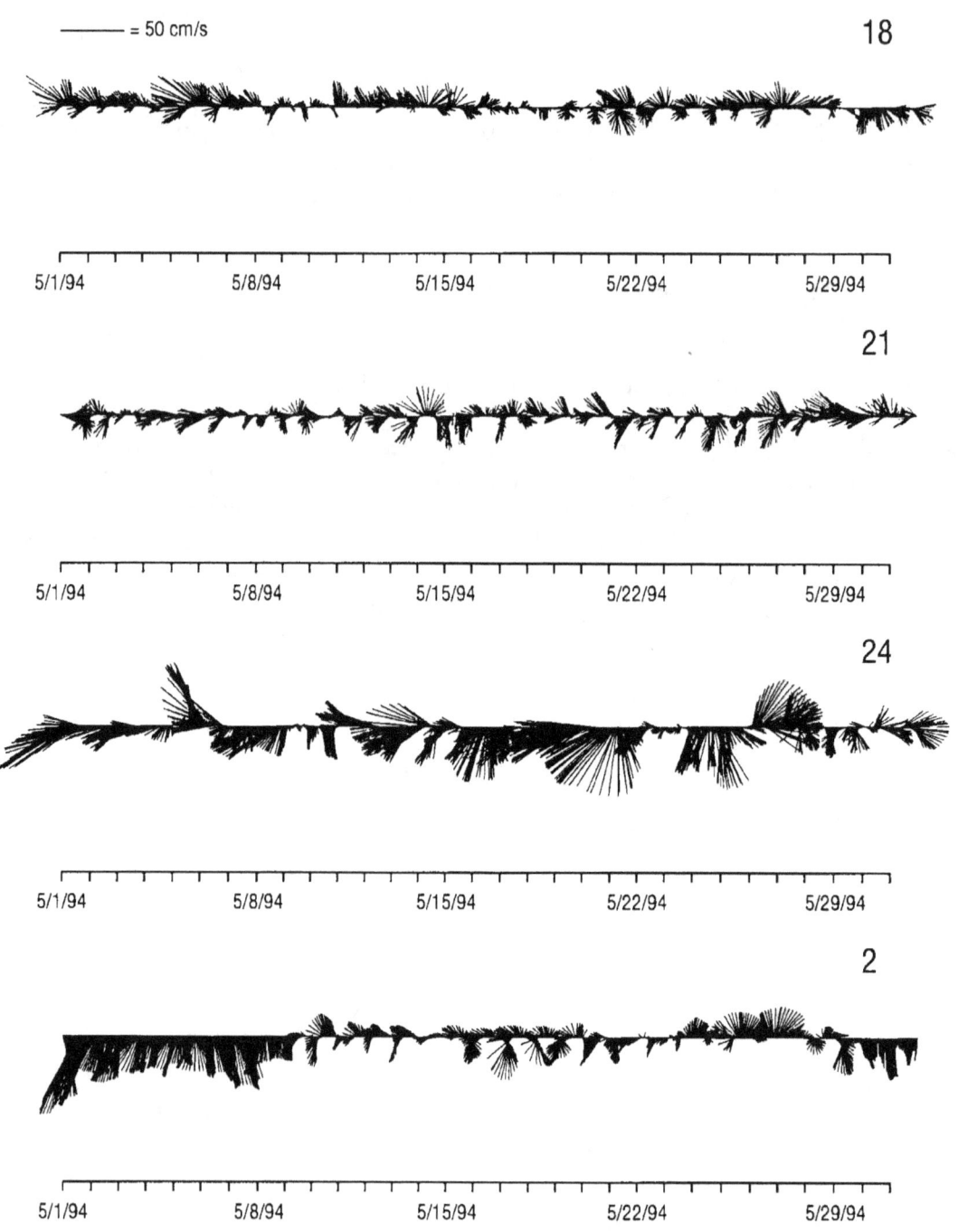

Figure 20. Stick vector representation of current meter data for moorings 18, 21, 24 and 2 for **(a) May1994**; (b) June 1994; (c) July 1994 and (d) August 1994. Vectors are plotted using standard oceanographic convention with northward currents pointing to top of page.

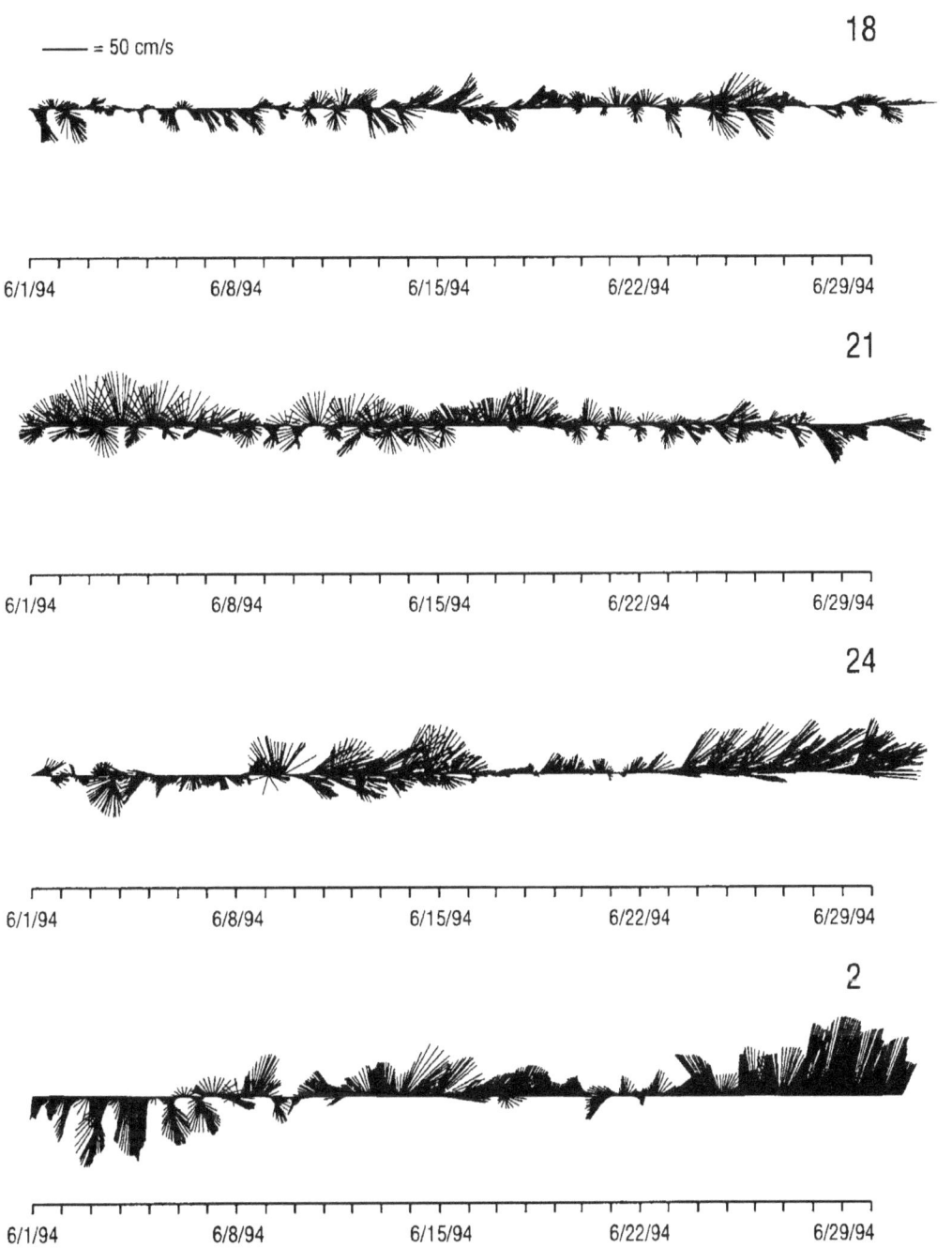

Figure 20 (continued). Stick vector representation of current meter data for moorings 18, 21, 24 and 2 for (a) May 1994; **(b) June 1994**; (c) July 1994 and (d) August 1994. Vectors are plotted using standard oceanographic convention with northward currents pointing to top of page.

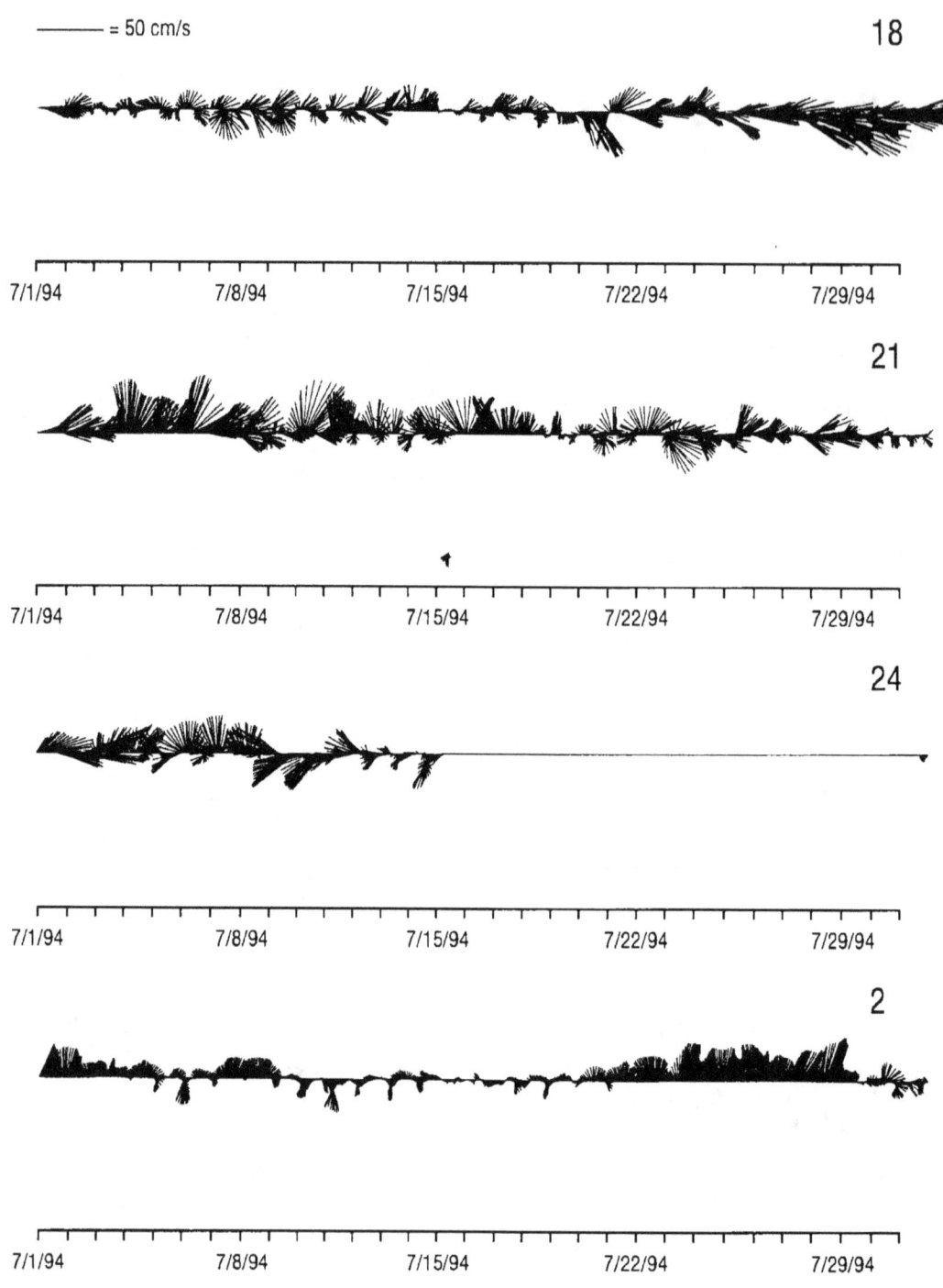

Figure 20 (continued). Stick vector representation of current meter data for moorings 18, 21, 24 and 2 for (a) May 1994; (b) June 1994; **(c) July 1994** and (d) August 1994. Vectors are plotted using standard oceanographic convention with northward currents pointing to top of page.

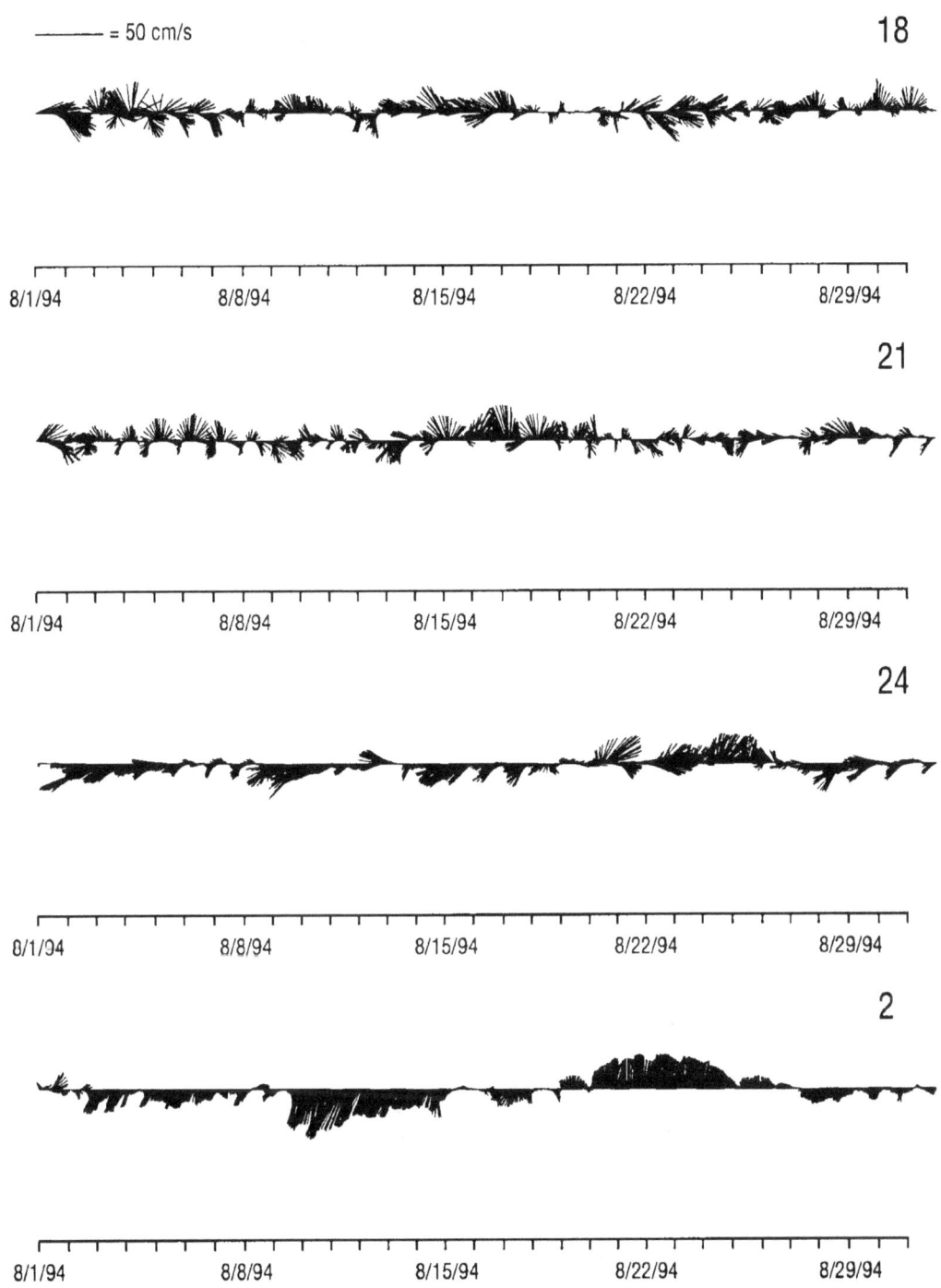

Figure 20 (continued). Stick vector representation of current meter data for moorings 18, 21, 24 and 2 for (a) May 1994; (b) June 1994; (c) July 1994 and **(d) August 1994**. Vectors are plotted using standard oceanographic convention with northward currents pointing to top of page.

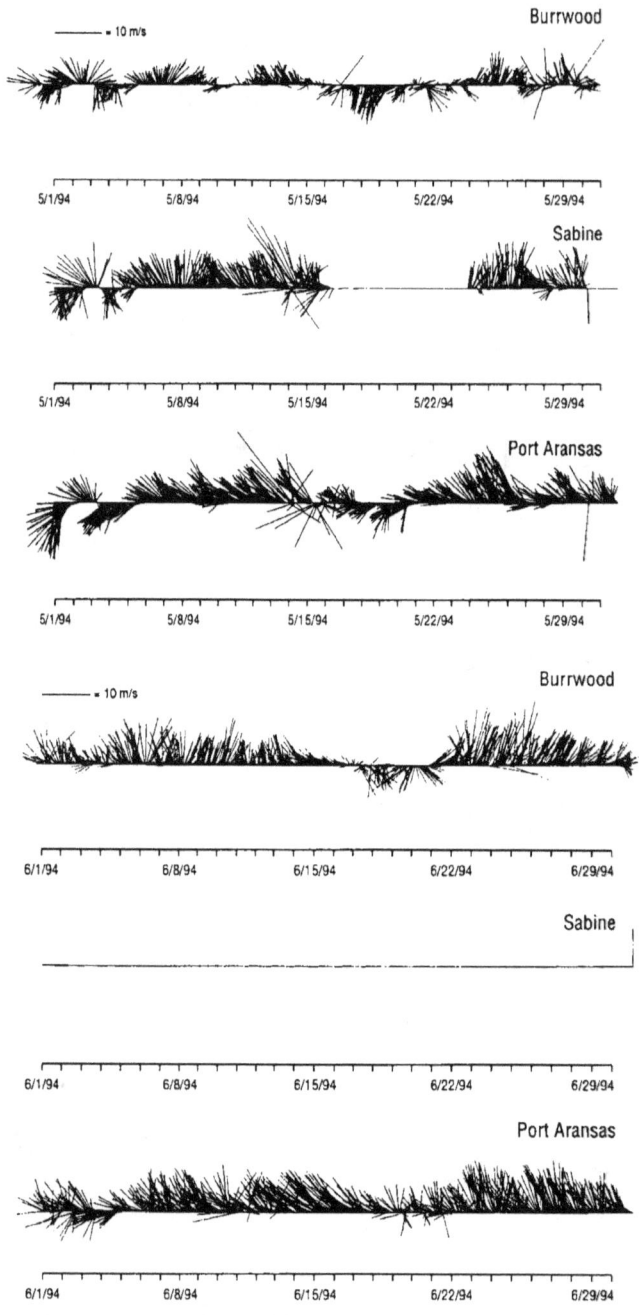

Figure 21. Stick vector representation of wind speed and direction data from Burrwood, LA; Sabine, TX and Port Aransas, TX for **(a) May 1994; (b) June 1994;** (c) July 1994 and (d) August 1994. Wind vectors are plotted using standard oceanographic orientation where winds blowing to the north point to the top of the page.

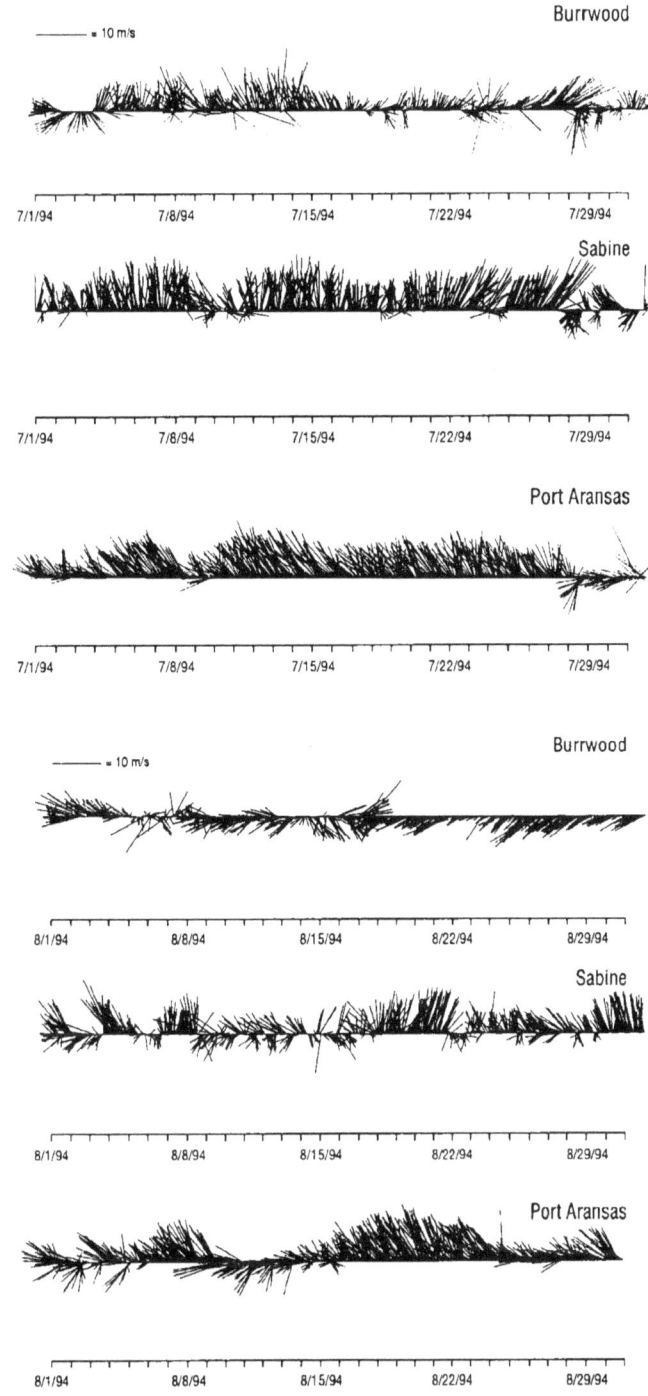

Figure 21 (continued). Stick vector representation of wind speed and direction data from Burrwood, LA; Sabine, TX and Port Aransas, TX for (a) May 1994; (b) June 1994; **(c) July 1994** and **(d) August 1994**. Wind vectors are plotted using standard oceanographic orientation where winds blowing to the north point to the top of the page.

45

4. Texas/Mexican Upwelling of Summer 1994

A sequence of three SST images from June 28, 1994 through July 26, 1994 are shown in Figure 22 to illustrate the spatial structure of the tongues of cold water due to upwelling along the Texas and Mexican coastlines and their evolution over time. The coldest coastal temperatures were observed in the June 28 image when a distinct band of relatively cool water (22-23° C) was observed to extend from 22° N to 29° N (near Galveston Bay). This image corresponded in time with the strongest up-coast current velocities along the Texas coastline (see moorings 2 and 24 in Figure 20). The northward component of the wind stress was maximized prior to image acquisition during the June 23-28 time period (Figure 21). The upwelling zone along the south Texas coast was observed as a cool coastal band extending about 20 km offshore. North of Matagorda Bay, the coastal upwelling was less continuous but filaments of cool upwelled water up to 50 km long were detected extending towards the east-northeast along the coast (Figure 22). The scale, orientation and longevity along the Mexican and Texas coastline indicates that the waters were upwelled locally rather than a result of river-runoff or advection from much further south.

By July 8, cold coastal waters were not in evidence north of Port Aransas, indicating that vigorous coastal upwelling had abated along the northern portion of the Texas coastline. The northward wind stress decreased during the period between these images. The imagery of July 8 did reveal the presence of recently upwelled waters (very cold) along the coast in the vicinity of moorings 1 and 2 and south of that along the Mexican coast. In addition, filaments of cool water were observed in the imagery between the 20 and 50 m isobaths probably as a result of advection away from the coast. By July 26, coastal upwelling had become more vigorous and was observed further north along the Texas coast (to 28° N). On July 8, an elongated filament of cool water extended from the Mexican coast near 24.5° N towards the north-northeast for 340 km (Figure 22). Advection of coastal water offshore is most likely attributable to the anticyclonic (clockwise) circulation around the warm core ring centered near 25.5° N and 95.5° W.

Temperatures from LATEX-A mooring 1 are shown in Figure 23 for three consecutive spring/summer seasons: 1992, 1993 and 1994. Water temperatures below 25° C were shaded to enable visual comparison of the intensity of upwelling. These data demonstrated that the wind-forced upwelling of summer along the Texas coast occurred primarily between mid-June and August. In the 1994 summer, the upwelling season lasted about five weeks and was intense with temperatures as low as 22° C at mooring 1 (Figure 23). The upwelling during 1992 and 1993 was persistent but temperatures were not as low as during 1994. A comparison of satellite imagery obtained for the three summers revealed that the upwelling zone extended farther north during the 1994 summer. Abnormally low summer temperatures were documented in Galveston Bay between June 25 and July 4, 1994 (Melinda Bailey, National Weather Service Forecast Office, New Braunfels, TX, personal communication). The minimum summer temperature of 23° C was recorded in Galveston Bay on June 30, 2 days after image acquisition. Typically, monthly averaged summer temperatures of 28-30 ° C (Figure 2) would be expected.

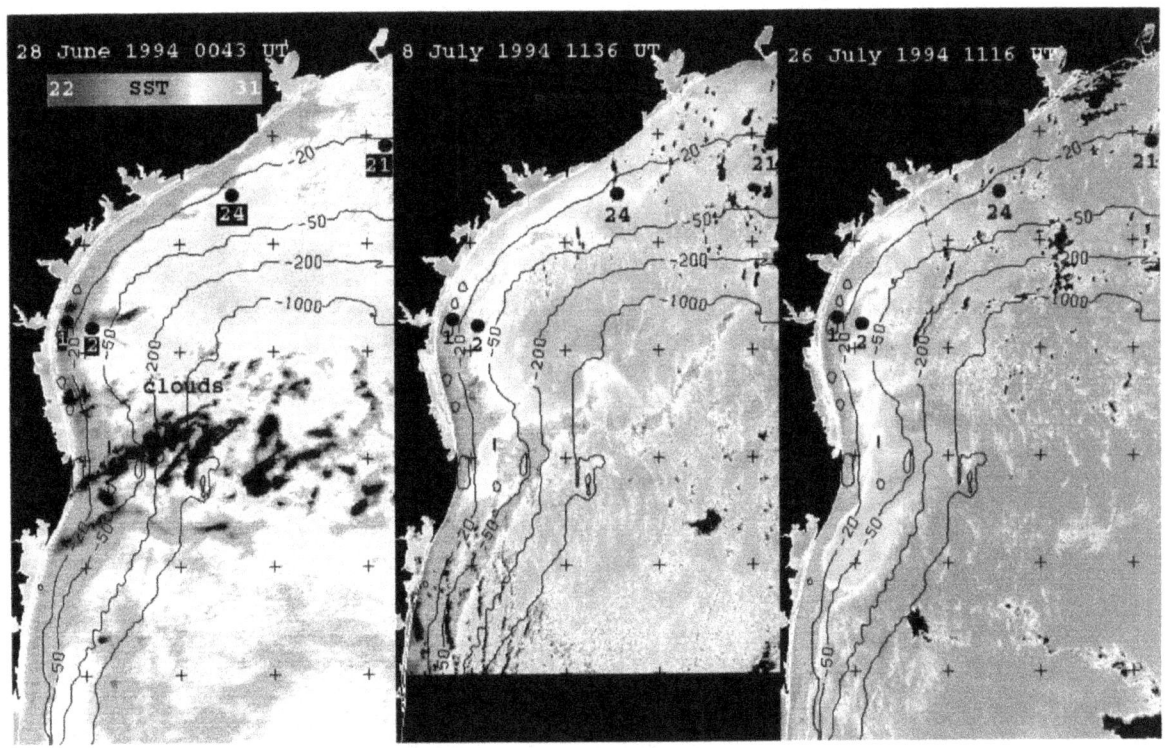

Figure 22. Sequence of 3 satellite images: June 28, July 8 and July 26, 1994 depicting the spatial extent of cool upwelled waters along the Texas coast (blue tones). The locations of LATEX moorings 1, 2, 24 and 21 are shown for reference purposes.

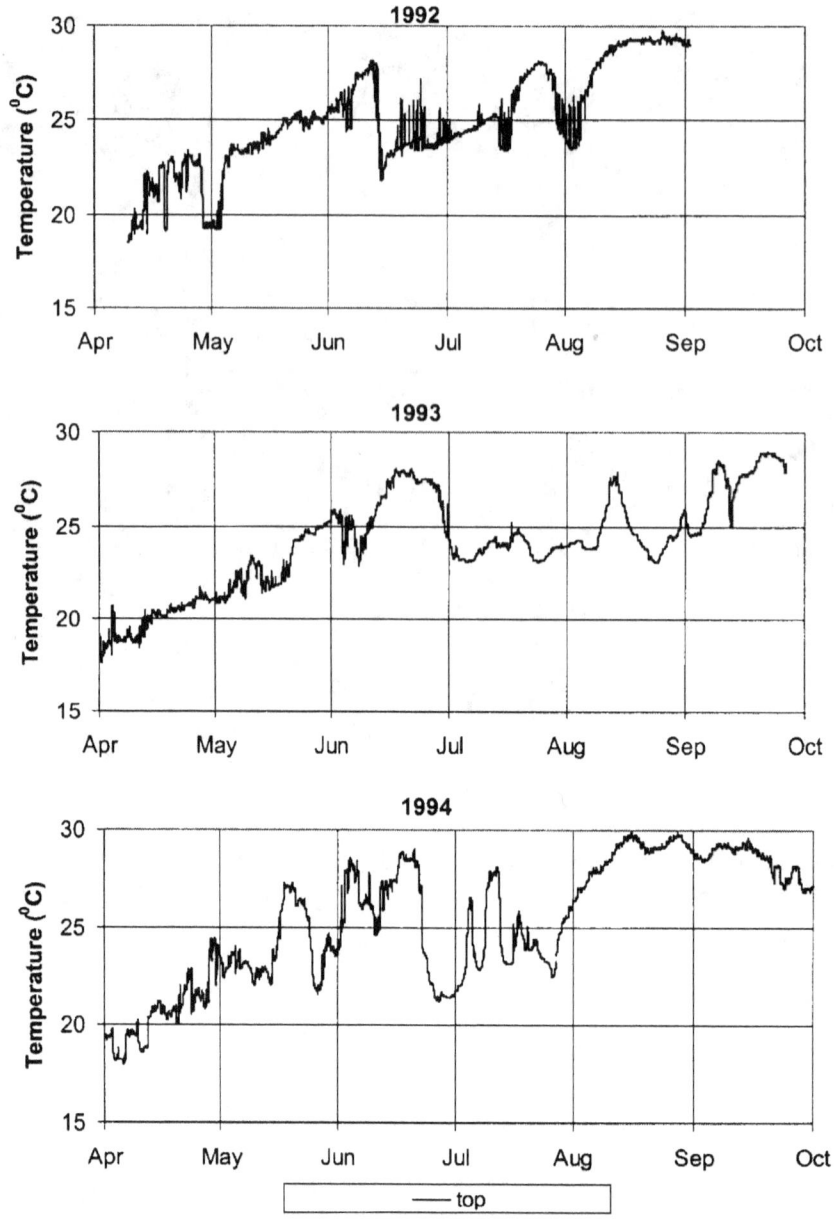

Figure 23. Water temperatures from mooring 1 (Location, Figure 22) (14 m deep, instrument was 10m from surface) during the April 1-September 30 time period for 3 consecutive years: 1992; 1993 and 1994.

IV. SUMMARY AND CONCLUSIONS

A. Autumn/Winter 1993/94 Temperature Changes and Frontal Formation

Cooling of inner shelf waters occurs rapidly in autumn as winter storms provide conditions that favor heat loss from the Gulf of Mexico waters into the atmosphere, primarily via the processes of evaporation and sensible heat loss. In addition, upwelling of bottom waters during west wind (upwelling favorable) wind events (associated with the passage of winter storms) could contribute to the rapid temperature changes. An additional source of cooling to the shelf is the introduction of Mississippi and Atchafalaya River waters along the Louisiana coast. Cooling of 12-15°C was experienced on the Louisiana and Texas inner shelf from late September to late November 1993. The coastal plume, extending from Atchafalaya Bay westward and along the Texas coast, was observed as a very cold water mass separated from the deeper waters by a distinct thermal front. This front of 3-5° C/ 10 km was located in close proximity to the 20 m isobath on November 28, 1993. It appeared to mark a convergence zone as drifters did not flow across this front. It is interesting to note that very few (2) drifters hit the Texas coastline from October through January of the study period out of a total released of 136. The LATEX-B autumn data indicates that temperature and salinity fronts associated with the coastal plume often coincide during the autumn/winter period.

The strongest SST fronts (4-6°C/10 km) were observed where Mississippi River waters abutted with relatively warm shelf waters southwest of the delta. Multiple fronts were observed seaward of Atchafalaya Bay, probably formed by the repetitive seaward flux of cool bay and shelf waters due to winter storms. The main shelf front along the Texas coast was located about 25 to 35 km from the coast in late autumn (Figure 4). It moved seaward from autumn to winter and in January the mid-point of the SST front was located between 40 to 55 km from the coast. The mid-Texas shelf region, represented by profile B was the site of substantial off-shelf advection of cool water that formed the Matagorda squirt on the outer shelf and slope in November and December 1993.

From late summer to mid-winter, the inner shelf cooled from 30° to 15°C. The outer shelf cooled from 31° to 22-24°C. The warmest shelf waters were detected in the region between the Mississippi and Atchafalaya river discharges.

B. Autumn/Winter 1993/94 Down-Coast Flow Regime

The results of this study demonstrate that circulation on the inner and mid-shelf regions of the Louisiana/Texas continental shelf is controlled primarily by wind forcing a result that concurs in general with previous studies (Cochrane and Kelly, 1986; Murray, 1998). Down-coast flow (from Louisiana to Texas and southward along the Texas coast) prevails during much of autumn, winter and spring due to the prevalence of westward wind stress. The orientation of flow is generally along the isobaths and, therefore changes from westward flow along the Louisiana shelf to southward flow along the Texas shelf when currents are down-coast. Velocities at the surface and down to about 10m are strongest when winds blow towards the southwest along the Louisiana coast and towards the south along the Texas coast. This wind stress situation occurs frequently with the intrusion of strong high pressure systems in the wake of cold-front passages. Down-coast current velocities are considerably stronger along the Texas coast as a result of the constriction in the continental shelf, moving from Louisiana to Texas, as discussed previously by Murray (1998). The strongest sustained near-surface flow was experienced at mooring 24 (on central Texas shelf) where maximum monthly velocities exceeded 70 cm/s during 7 months of the 11-month analysis period (Table 3). The mean velocities over this period were 22 cm/s. Current velocities at mooring 2 farther south were a little weaker than at mooring 24, however, maximum monthly velocities exceeded 60 cm/s during 6 months of the study period. The velocities on the Louisiana inner shelf were much lower than those on the Texas inner shelf. These mooring measurements may actually under-estimate velocities within the coastal current since the instruments may have been seaward and/or deeper than the main axis of the coastal plume (Murray, 1998).

Figure 24 depicts sub-tidal along-coast flow at moorings 2 (north/south component) and 21 (east-west component) for the October 93-January 94 period. It is clearly evident that down-coast flow predominated during this time period with strongest currents along the Texas coast. Flow was fairly coherent across the shelf and strongest flow coincided with southward and southwestward winds along the Louisiana and Texas shelf, respectively. Current reversals were experienced several times during this time period. There were five main periods of up-coast flow at mooring 21 and these up-coast flow events also occurred at mooring 2. The wind records demonstrate that the up-coast flow along the Texas coast coincided with the strong northward wind stress events. The up-coast flow along the Louisiana coast resulted from eastward winds that blew in advance of cold-front passages.

C. Impacts of Warm Core Rings and Eddy Pairs on Shelf Circulation

The synthesis of clear sky satellite SST data and SSH data enabled a better evaluation of the circulation features that influenced the movement of SCULP drifters during autumn and winter 1993/94. In particular, the close proximity of three warm core rings and several cold core eddies to the Louisiana/Texas shelf edge impacted upon circulation of the drifters. The movement of these features over time altered surface circulation processes on the shelf. Of particular interest was the identification of a narrow off-shelf flow regime southeast from Matagorda Bay. This flow regime observed primarily in November and December 1993 was termed the Matagorda squirt. Approximately 40% of the drifters released in October and November 1993 experienced off-shelf advection within this squirt feature. In the satellite SST data, the feature was revealed as a streamer of relatively cool water extending between the 30m to 200 m isobath. The feature formed between a warm core ring (Eddy V/W) to the south and a cold core eddy on the shelf to the north. Daily-averaged velocities of the drifters averaged 39 cm/s and ranged from 19 to 59 cm/s in water depths between 50 and 1000 m (Table 2). Subsequent drifter movement around the warm core ring were slightly higher, averaging 45 cm/s with maximum velocities reaching 75 cm/s. During December 1993, only 30% of the drifters were advected into this feature and by January the feature had disappeared. The SSH data demonstrated that the warm core ring moved away from the shelf, removing the main source of the forcing for this flow regime. This interesting case study reveals the large impact that warm core rings can have on shelf circulation, even away from the shelf edge. This observation concurs with the modeling results of Oey (1995) that showed the eastward shelf edge current is caused by the collision of warm core rings with the shelf.

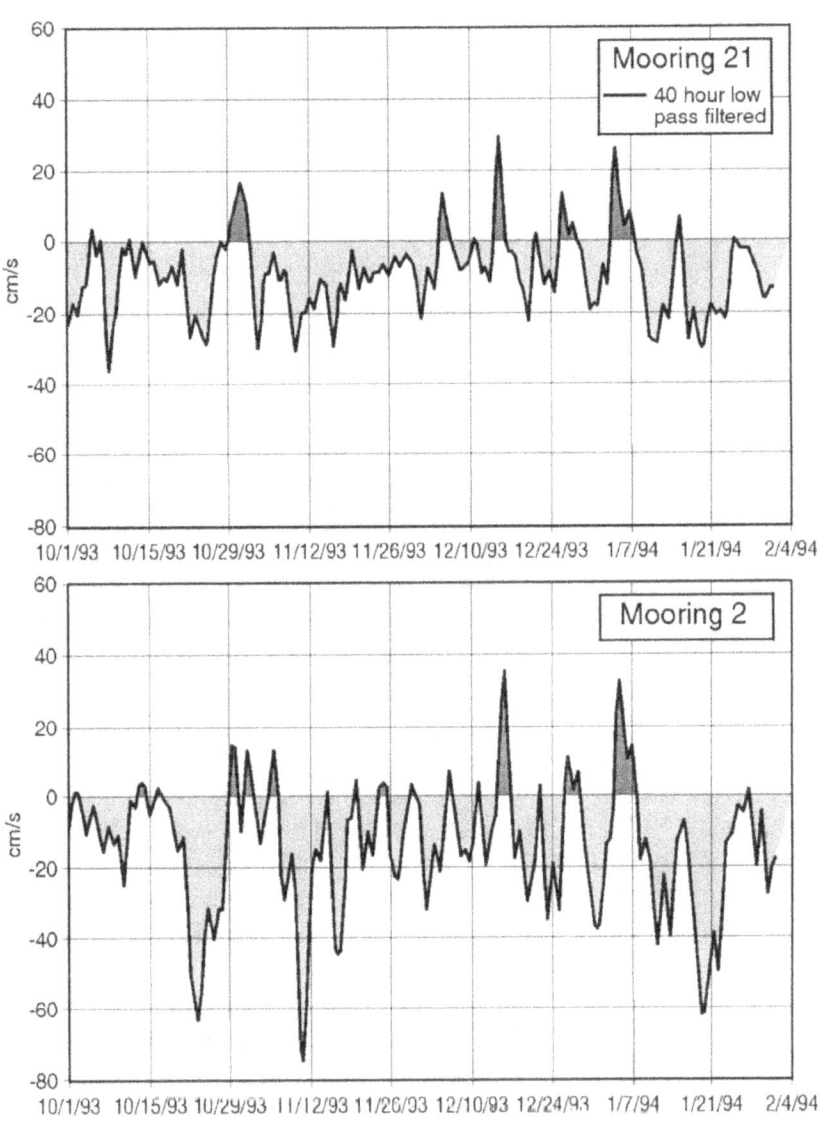

Figure 24. De-tided along-shelf components of currents, from October 1, 1993 to January 31, 1994, at mooring 21 (east-west component, east positive) and mooring 2 (north-south component, north positive). Contrasting shading was applied to the up-coast and down-coast flows.

During the autumn/winter 1993/4, a warm core ring (Eddy W) was located in close proximity to the Mexican shelf with a center near 24° N latitude (Figure 12). By mid-December 1993, a cold core eddy was located north of it (Figure 12). Approximately 21% of the coastal current drifters that entered Mexican waters between October and January were advected seaward within a narrow squirt that formed between this eddy pair (Figure 13). Daily-averaged surface velocities ranged from 13-55 cm/s with a mean of 36 cm/s (Table 2). A clear-sky sequence of satellite imagery (December 14-January 8) and simultaneous drifter data enabled the detection of circulation changes associated with the eddy pair. The squirt advected a substantial body of relatively cool shelf water seaward that eventually moved onto the slope, measuring 20,000 km^2 at the surface. Of particular note was the detection of a rapid northeastward

51

movement of the eddy and squirt that corresponded roughly in time with the southeastward movement of the warm core ring away from the Texas shelf edge. These observations are testimony to the rapidity with which slope circulation changes occur in the NW GOM.

D. The Summer Up-Coast Flow Regime

The quasi-isothermal shelf temperature structure of spring (Figure 15) is replaced by a very different surface temperature distribution in summer. Northward wind stress along the Texas coast results in a coastally extensive band of cool waters, 20-30 km wide, extending from Mexico to Matagorda Bay (Figure 22). These cool waters contrast with the warm surface waters typical of the rest of the Louisiana/Texas shelf (Figure 17). During June 1994, upwelling was stronger than normal and coastal upwelling was detected along the entire Texas coast from 26°N to Galveston (Figure 22). The satellite SST imagery reveals that the cool coastal waters move towards the northeast with the general up-coast shelf flow along the Texas coast. Warm core eddies on the slope typically advect the cool upwelled waters seaward into the deeper GOM (See Figure 22, middle panel). Water temperatures below 25°C are commonly experienced along the Texas coast during June and July and sometimes August (Figure 23). The severity of the cooling and the longevity of upwelling is controlled primarily by the intensity and longevity of the northward wind stress. Figure 25 depicts the sub-tidal currents at moorings 2 and 21 during the May1-August 31, 1994 time period. The most long-lived and pronounced up-coast flow events at both sites occurred in late June/early July and in late July. An additional event similar to the July event was experienced at Mooring 2 in late August. The lowest water temperatures recorded at mooring 1 (Figure 23) corresponded with the strongest up-coast flow at moorings 2 and 21 (Figure 25). Along-shore sub-tidal velocities of 40-50 cm/s were experienced from south Texas to the Louisiana shelf during the strongest period of strong northward winds in summer 1994.

The data analyzed indicate that the summer up-coast flow regime is regionally extensive across the Louisiana/Texas shelf. There was no evidence of a surface convergence zone in summer between the up-coast flow regime along the south Texas coast and a down-coast flow regime from Louisiana. In fact, the data show that at 10 m depth up-coast flow (to north and east) occurred first along the northern Texas and central Louisiana shelf. Comparison of drifter data with sub-surface mooring data clearly demonstrate that the surface flow responds within hours to wind events whereas the sub-surface flow can exhibit lag times of days to weeks, especially along the south Texas coast. The up-coast flow regime of summer is relatively short-lived compared with the predominant down-coast flow regime of autumn, winter and spring.

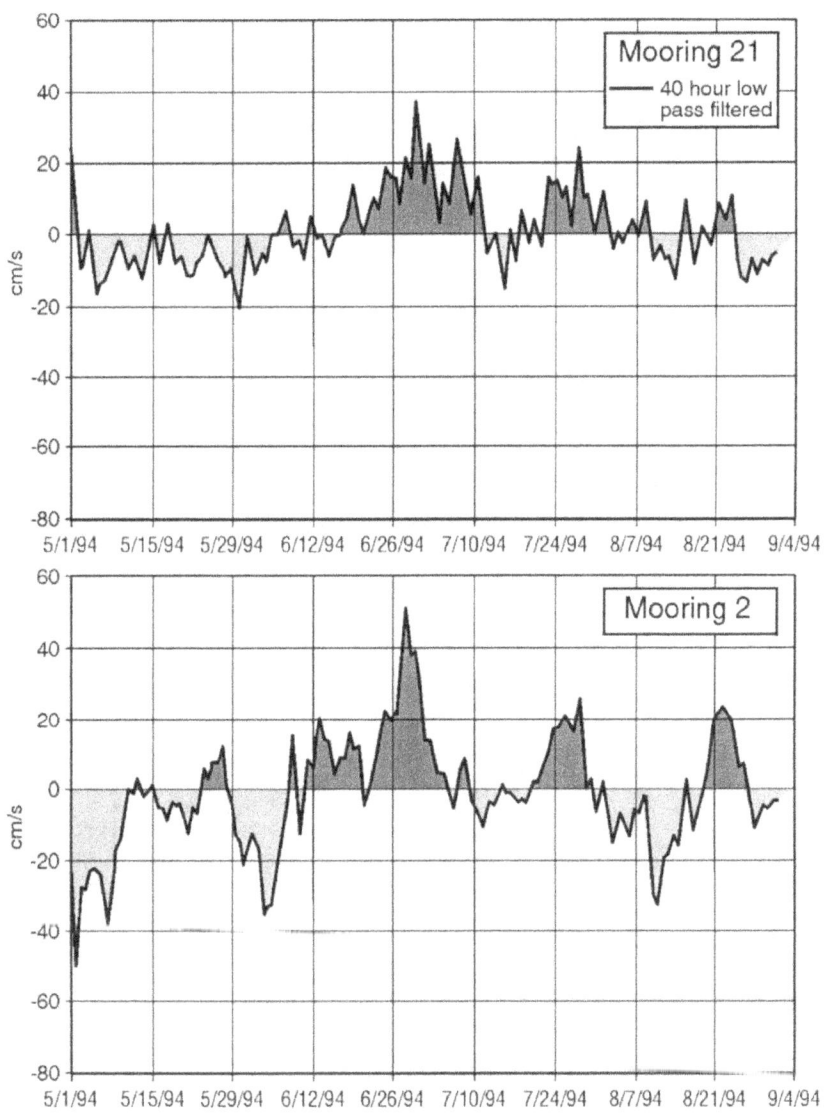

Figure 25. De-tided along-shelf components of currents, from May 1 to August 31, 1994, at mooring 21 (east-west component, east positive) and mooring 2 (north-south component, north positive). Contrasting shading was applied to the up-coast and down-coast flows.

V. REFERENCES

Barron, C.N. and A.C. Vastano. 1994. Satellite observations of surface circulation in the northwestern Gulf of Mexico during March and April 1989. Continental Shelf Research. 14: 607-628.

Biggs, D. C. 1992. Nutrients, plankton, and productivity in a warm-core ring in the western Gulf of Mexico. Journal of Geophysical Research. 97: 2143-2154.

Biggs, D.C., G.S. Fargion, P. Hamilton, and R.R. Leben. 1996. Cleavage of a Gulf of Mexico Loop Current eddy by a deep water cyclone. Journal of Geophysical Research. 101: 20,629-20,641.

Brooks, D.A. and R.V. Legeckis. 1982. A ship and satellite view of hydrographic features in the western Gulf of Mexico. Journal of Geophysical Research. 87: 4195-4206.

Cochrane, J.D. 1972. Separation of an anticyclone and subsequent developments in the Loop Current (1969), in *Contributions on the Physical Oceanography of the Gulf of Mexico*, Tex. A&M Univ Oceanographic Studies Vol 2, edited by L.R.A. Capurro and J.L. Reid, 91-106. Gulf: Houston, Texas.

Cochrane, J.D. and F.J. Kelley. 1986. Low-frequency circulation on the Texas-Louisiana continental shelf. Journal of Geophysical Research. 91: 10,645-10,659.

Cooper, C., G.Z. Forristall, and T.M. Joyce. 1990. Velocity and hydrographic structure of two Gulf of Mexico warm-core rings. Journal of Geophysical Research. 95: 1663-1679.

Crout, R.L., W.J. Wiseman, Jr., and W.S. Chuang. 1984. Variability of wind-driven currents, west Louisiana inner continental shelf. Contributions to Marine Science. 27: 1-11.

Elliot, B.A. 1982. Anticyclonic rings in the Gulf of Mexico. Journal of Physical Oceanography, 12: 1293-1309.

Forristall, G.Z., K.J. Schaudt, C.K. Cooper. 1992. Evolution and kinematics of a Loop Current eddy in the Gulf of Mexico during 1985. Journal of Geophysical Research. 97: 2173-2184.

Hamilton, P. 1992. Lower continental slope cyclonic eddies in the central Gulf of Mexico. Journal of Geophysical Research. 97: 2185-2200.

Hsu, S.A. 1988. Coastal Meteorology. Academic: San Diego, California.

Huh, O.K., Wiseman, W.J., Jr., and Rouse, L.J., Jr. 1978. Winter cycle of sea surface thermal patterns: Northeastern Gulf of Mexico. Journal of Geophysical Research. 83: 523-4529.

Huh, O.K. and Schaudt, K.J. 1990. Satellite imagery tracks currents in Gulf of Mexico. Oil and Gas Journal. 88: 70-76.

Jarosz, E., S.P. Murray, P.S. Niiler, E.T. Weeks, C.E. Ebbesmeyer. 1996. Comparison of ADCP and drifter observations of circulation in the Louisiana-Texas coastal current, summer 1994, *EOS,* Transactions, American Geophysical Union. 76:3: OS98, Ocean Sciences Conference, San Diego, California.

Johnson, W.R. and P.P. Niiler. 1994. SCULP drifter study in the Northwest Gulf of Mexico. American Geophysical Union, Fall Meeting, San Francisco. O52C-8.

Leben, R.R., G.H. Born, D.C. Biggs, D.R. Johnson, and N.D. Walker. 1993. Verification of TOPEX altimetry in the Gulf of Mexico. TOPEX/POSEIDON Research News. 1, 3-8.

Lewis, J.K. and A.D. Kirwan. 1985. Some observations of ring topography and ring-ring interactions in the Gulf of Mexico. Journal of Geophysical Research. 90: 9017-9028.

Lewis, J.K. and R.O. Reid. 1985. Local wind forcing of a coastal sea at subinertial frequencies. Journal of Geophysical Research. 90: 934-944.

Maul, F.A. and F.M. Vukovich. 1993. The relationship between variations in the Gulf of Mexico Loop Current and Straits of Florida volume transport. Journal of Physical Oceanography. 23: 785-7.

McClain, E.P., W.G. Pichel, and C.C. Walton. 1985. Comparative performance of AVHRR-based multi-channel sea surface temperatures. Journal of Geophysical Research. 90: 11,587-11,601.

Merrell, W.J., Jr. and J. Morrison. 1981. On the circulation of the western Gulf of Mexico with observations from April 1978. Journal of Geophysical Research. 86: 4181-4185.

Murray, S.P. 1998. An observational study of the Mississippi-Atchafalaya coastal plume: Final report. OCS Study MMS 98-0040. U.S. Dept. of the Interior, Minerals Mgmt. Service, Gulf of Mexico OCS Region, New Orleans, Louisiana. 513 pp.

Nowlin, W.D. and C.A. Parker. 1974. Effects of a cold-air outbreak on shelf waters of the Gulf of Mexico. Journal of Geophysical Research. 4: 467-486.

Nowlin, W.D., A.E. Jochens, R.O. Reid, and S.F. DiMarco. 1998. Texas-Louisiana Shelf Circulation and Transport Processes Study: Synthesis Report. Volume I: Technical Report. OCS Study MMS 98-0035. U.S. Dept. of the Interior, Minerals Management Service, Gulf of Mexico OCS Region, New Orleans, LA 502 pp.

Oey, L.-Y. 1995. Eddy and wind-forced shelf circulation. Journal of Geophysical Research. 100: 8621-8637.

Rhodes, R.C., A.J. Wallcraft, and J.D. Thompson. 1985. Navy-corrected geostrophic wind set for the Gulf of Mexico. NORDA Technical Note 310. Stennis Space Center, MS. 103 pp.

Rouse, L.J. and J.M. Coleman. 1976. Circulation observations in the Louisiana Bight using LANDSAT imagery. Remote Sensing of Environment. XL: 635-642.

Smith, N.P. 1978. Low-frequency reversals of nearshore currents in the north-western Gulf of Mexico. Contributions to Marine Science. 21: 103-115.

Smith, N.P. 1980. Temporal and spatial variability in longshore motion along the Texas Gulf Coast. Journal of Geophysical Research. 85: 1531-1536.

Sturges, W. 1994. The frequency of ring separations from the Loop Current. Journal of Physical Oceanography., 24: 1647-1651.

Vidal, V.M., F.V. Vidal, and J.M. Perez-Molero. 1992. Collision of a Loop Current Anticyclonic ring against the continental shelf slope of the western Gulf of Mexico. Journal of Geophysical Research. 97: 2155-2172.

Walker, N.D. and Rouse, L.J. Jr. 1993. Satellite assessment of Mississippi River discharge plume variability. U.S. Dept. of the Interior, Minerals Management Service, Gulf of Mexico OCS Region, New Orleans, Louisiana. OCS Study MMS 93-0044. 50 pp.

Walker, N.D., G. Fargion, L.J. Rouse, Jr., and D. Biggs. 1994. The Great Flood of Summer 1993: Mississippi River discharge studied, EOS, Transactions, American Geophysical Union. 75:36: 409-415.

Walker, N.D. 1996. Satellite assessment of Mississippi River plume variability: Causes and predictability. Remote Sensing of Environment. 58: 21-35.

Walker, N.D., O.K. Huh, L.J. Rouse, Jr. and S.P. Murray. 1996. Evolution and structure of a coastal squirt off the Mississippi River Delta: Northern Gulf of Mexico. Journal of Geophysical Research. 101: 20,643-20,665.

Walker, N. and A. Hammack. 2000. Impacts of winter storms on circulation and sediment transport: Atchafalaya-Vermilion Bay region, Louisiana, USA. Journal of Coastal Research. 16: 996-1010.

Watson, R. and E.W. Behrens. 1970. Nearshore surface currents, southeastern Texas Gulf coast, *Contributions to Marine Science*. 15: 133-143.

The Department of the Interior Mission

As the Nation's principal conservation agency, the Department of the Interior has responsibility for most of our nationally owned public lands and natural resources. This includes fostering sound use of our land and water resources; protecting our fish, wildlife, and biological diversity; preserving the environmental and cultural values of our national parks and historical places; and providing for the enjoyment of life through outdoor recreation. The Department assesses our energy and mineral resources and works to ensure that their development is in the best interests of all our people by encouraging stewardship and citizen participation in their care. The Department also has a major responsibility for American Indian reservation communities and for people who live in island territories under U.S. administration.

The Minerals Management Service Mission

As a bureau of the Department of the Interior, the Minerals Management Service's (MMS) primary responsibilities are to manage the mineral resources located on the Nation's Outer Continental Shelf (OCS), collect revenue from the Federal OCS and onshore Federal and Indian lands, and distribute those revenues.

Moreover, in working to meet its responsibilities, the **Offshore Minerals Management Program** administers the OCS competitive leasing program and oversees the safe and environmentally sound exploration and production of our Nation's offshore natural gas, oil and other mineral resources. The MMS **Royalty Management Program** meets its responsibilities by ensuring the efficient, timely and accurate collection and disbursement of revenue from mineral leasing and production due to Indian tribes and allottees, States and the U.S. Treasury.

The MMS strives to fulfill its responsibilities through the general guiding principles of: (1) being responsive to the public's concerns and interests by maintaining a dialogue with all potentially affected parties and (2) carrying out its programs with an emphasis on working to enhance the quality of life for all Americans by lending MMS assistance and expertise to economic development and environmental protection.

www.ingramcontent.com/pod-product-compliance
Lightning Source LLC
Chambersburg PA
CBHW052010280526
45793CB00005B/919